THE AFTERMATH:

WITH

Autobiography of the Author

JOHN BEDFORD LENO.

LONDON:
PUBLISHED BY REEVES & TURNER,
196 STRAND, W.C.

1892.

CONTENTS.

AUTOBIOGRAPHY.

Autobiography of John Bedford Leno 1

THE AFTERMATH.

A Tale of Severn Side	1	Give me the Stream	27
The Ruined Castle	8	A Fragment	28
Jim's Story	9	Long Ago	28
After the Battle of Hastings	10	Recollections of Home	28
		Snow Flakes	29
The Last Battle (A.D. 2000)	12	Hunt the Slipper	29
		The Rival Chieftains	30
Divine Right	15	A Love Story	31
St. Crispin	16	Lily Lovelace	32
The French Bootmakers' Challenge	18	Love's Message	32
		A Story for Yule Tide	33
The Reply	19	She Came in the Golden Summer Time	34
The Ballet Girl	20		
The Village Dorcas	21	The Last Dream	34
The Age of the World	22	Only a Dreamer	35
Shakespeare	22	Over a Century	36
Joy and Sorrow	22	The Ploughing Match	37
Spring and Summer	23	The Widow's Luck	37
Autumn and Winter	23	A Lay Sarmint	39
The Sea Nymph's Home	24	A Tale of a Dog	40
A Simile	24	The Farm-Yard Nightingale	41
Art	24		
The Sick Clown and the Lost Letter	25	A Second Sketch of Kimburton	41
Alderman Stubbs	26	Swapping Horses	42

HISTORICAL POEMS RELATING TO UXBRIDGE AND ITS NEIGHBOURHOOD.

The Treaty of Uxbridge	1	Down Where the Mill Stream Meanders	10
Ye Woxbrugge Tolle Riot (1631)	2	Clear as Crystal Flows the Colne	11
The Lynch Martyrs (1555)	3		
The Mound on the Moor	5	Herne's Oak	11
The History of Gerard Cross	6	On the Ruins of Reading Abbey	12
The Battle of Bulstrode in 1066	7	The Gospel Oak	12
		To my Mother	13
The Rose of Swakeley	9	Our Old Town	13
The Old Hollow Tree	10	My Old Home at Uxbridge	14
By the Margin of the Colne	10	Billy the Sweep	15
		Notes to the Poems	16

Errata.—In line 9 of the text life opposite for "was then," read "were."

DEDICATED

TO THE MEMBERS

OF

THE HOTSPUR CLUB,

IN RECOGNITION

OF

THEIR KINDNESS TO ME

DURING MY PROLONGED ILLNESS.

JOHN BEDFORD LENO.

UXBRIDGE, 1892.

AUTOBIOGRAPHY OF
JOHN BEDFORD LENO.

I WAS born on the 29th of June, 1826, at No. 14 Bell Yard, Uxbridge, Middlesex. At this period this row of cottages, forming the upper yard, had not long been built, and must have presented an air of comfort and decency that has long since vanished. Each house consisted of four rooms, two on the ground floor, and two above; and stretching along the entire row was a narrow strip of meadow land, forming an excellent playground for the children dwelling on the spot. The inhabitants of this row of houses was then, and are now, confined to working men, their wives, and families. During a recent visit to my native town, I was horrified by the squalor and misery that characterised the houses of which my birthplace forms a part, and the contrast between Bell Yard in past days and the present was certainly not indicative of improvement. As I peered into cottage after cottage, the conviction strengthened that here at least the condition of the town had not improved.

White-sanded floors, polished chairs and tables, in a word, well-cared-for homes were few and far between; neither did the children appear to be so well looked after as formerly. Lest I should be accused of want of fairness, I admit that the drainage and water supply have been improved, but withal, possibly from the extreme poverty of the inhabitants, the interiors of the houses in this yard, on the ground of decency and cleanliness, are not to be compared with what they were in bygone days, and, with regard to their exteriors, it may be noted that the vine and apricot trees that once spread over the house fronts have long since disappeared. This, to me, is a matter of great regret. The sight of the change recalled forcibly to my mind a notable speech of England's greatest statesman, wherein he took occasion to direct the attention of the poorer classes of his countrymen to the necessity of cultivating and preserving fruit as a source of both income and thrift. In one instance, it may be recorded, the average yield of a single apricot tree was not less than £9, a sum equal to the rent of the house over the front of which it spread.

My grandfather was born at King's Langley, in Hertfordshire, where he was taught the trade of a wheel-wright. At an unusually early age he married the daughter of a well-to-do farmer, named Jackson, who dwelt within a short distance of the site of Old Verulam. His father having removed to Uxbridge, he accompanied him there, where, on his father's death, he took up his position as landlord of the "Catherine Wheel," in Cross Street. Here he lived, and died at the age of thirty-one, leaving behind him a widow and four young children. His relict, it would appear, soon tiring of her widowhood, took unto herself a second husband, named Baker, who quickly made ducks and drakes of the widow and children's patrimony.

In consequence of the discomfort which arose from the appearance of the second family, my father, his sister, and his brother Mathew, quitted home, the youngest son having been drowned whilst sliding. While my father was engaged as a gentleman's servant, he became acquainted with Phœbe Bedford, a native of Stanwell Moor, near Staines, Middlesex. My maternal grandfather was a gardener at the "Bush Inn," and his wife a native of the principality of Wales. I have often heard my mother tell a story respecting her, which may be deemed worthy of repetition. When living with her parents in the principality, she had an offer of service in England. Being doubtful whether to accept it or not, she determined to consult some Welsh oracle, whose name I have forgotten. The accepted mode of doing this was to raise a stick perpendicularly, and when loosened, if it fell, as in this case, towards England, to accept the offer; if otherwise reject it. The stick fell Englandward, and, accordingly, to England she came. This incident decided my being. The name borne by me is either of Greek or Roman origin, but whether its early possessor who first made his appearance in this country came here to fight Boadicea, or to exhibit white mice, is unknown. Leno is the name of a portion of the brain, an animal of the tiger species, and the Italian name for linseed, which is said to be identical with the plant from which the gopher wood was derived, and from which the ark was built. My old friend, Thornton Hunt, the son of Leigh Hunt, first made me acquainted with the fact that one bearing the same surname was accused of plundering the treasury of ancient Rome, and that at the time of his making that fact known to me some one had written a book to prove that the accusation was false, and proceeded from malice begot by political prejudice. In addition to this, my uncle, Matthew Leno, of Staines, was told at Doctors' Commons that the names of Leno, Leno's, and Lennox were the same, and that Leno's was the family name of a former Duke of Richmond, who, I learn from Burke's "Extinct Peerage," was the son of an Italian courtezan, by the then king. This pleased the old gentleman mightily, and, whatever the cost the pedigree may have been, he thought it cheap at the price. For my part, it has always struck me that if it could be satisfactorily proved that I was the descendant of a monkey, it would be far more to my credit. The Herald's College decided that the family crest of the Leno's consisted of three shells, which, for fear of the tax, I have never caused to have had engraved on the family plate!

For the first eight or ten years of my life all went on smoothly. My father, for the whole of that period, was footman to a Mr. Chippendale, then well-known in the neighbourhood of Uxbridge as a true and disinterested philanthropist. In the same family, my mother, for several years previous, and up to the time of her marriage, acted as lady's maid. A footman's wages in those days were not large; but, no matter the precise amount, it, with my mother's earnings, served to keep us moderately well. The sources of my mother's contribution were needle-work and a dame school. I am afraid her scholastic qualifications would fail to commend her to the School Board authorities of to-day. In those days, however, a little education among the extremely poor went a long way, and as all her scholars were of tender years, the chief thing required from her was the power to interest them in all she professed to teach, and this power she possessed to a remarkable extent. Moreover, she had full control over her temper, and, no matter how dull or stupid the child she was teaching, she never impressed or advertised to her scholar a sense of her impatience or weariness.

To my mother, I attribute my love of learning, and under her care I made considerable progress. At ten years of age I was sent to the National School, but there I made no headway whatever, nor is this to be wondered at, when the slovenly system then in vogue there is remembered. When I had reached the age of twelve, or possibly before, it became necessary that I should do a something by way of contributing to the income of the household. The immediate cause of this change was my father leaving his situation. This resulted from his giving offence to a notoriously drunken parson of Iver, a supposed great friend of my father's then employer. I well remember the occasion, and how his late master begged for him to go back. Nothing, however, could induce my father to break a vow that he had made—that he would never wear any clothes but his own in future. His successor received a pension of 30s. a week on the death of the master which occurred within a twelvemonth of his entering the service.

I am sorry to have to confess that my father was robbed of his crested and plated buttons by his eldest son. On learning that they were missing, I was hastily summoned and charged with being the culprit. This ended in my own clothing being made to fit tighter than was plesant.

I could not have been more than eight years of age when I was sent to the preparatory school of a Mr. Moore. From this

I was speedily turned out upon the charge of having told a falsehood. This charge was totally untrue. The master had announced, so at least I understood him, that schooling would be discontinued for a week. This I communicated to my parents, and kept at home for the interval. On my return at its termination, I was sent home, notwithstanding my persistent assertion that I had not wilfully told an untruth. But I was and am convinced that the true explanation of this was that my presence was not required. It had become known that I hailed from Bell Yard, and it was thought by a few of the better off scholars that to associate with an inhabitant of so poor a quarter was degrading, and hence the reason for my master getting quit of me.

Shortly after I was packed off to my maternal aunt, Sutton, where I earned my keep by turning cow-minder in the neighbouring lanes. Never did I feel more proud than when my aunt consented to buy me a smock frock, and never more disappointed than when I discovered that it had only one pocket and was destitute of pleats in the front. At this period my uncle and aunt were in charge of the parish poor house in which they had apartments. The inmates were a queer lot, and I well remember that the spoons, knives, and plates were chained to the tables. I had charge of two cows beyond those belonging to my aunt, for the minding of which I received three shillings per week, which was devoted to my support. My sole ambition at that time was to become a ploughboy, a dignity which I fortunately never reached. When last at Stanwell Moor, I noticed that the grassy margins to its lanes have been incorporated into the adjoining fields, which, if I mistake not, is a barefaced robbery of the poor who used to profit by allowing their cows to feed thereon. This act is akin to the removal of the bequeathment tablet from the pillar of the parish church, which was taken down upon the plea of its ugliness. This may have been a just plea for what I know to the contrary; but it appears strange that the gift it published has gone with it. A deceased parson and deceased neighbouring Knight were credited with this piece of ætheticism!

Curious as it may seem, my first situation after leaving my aunt, was with the identical Mr. Moore from whose school I had been expelled. I was engaged to clean knives and forks, polish boots and shoes, and run errands, my wage being sixpence per week and a daily breakfast. This consisted chiefly of the leavings of the boarders, usually half mouldy. Strange as it may seem, I was the innocent cause of ruining this school. Through sympathy with a poor boy who was being taunted with having a contagious skin disease, I was elected to decide whether he was rightly or wrongly so charged. I was totally ignorant of the infection, but with assumed knowledge, I undertook my task. My decision was that the lad was wrongfully accused. In a short time after, I had cause to learn my mistake; but, in the meantime I had communicated it to the bulk of the scholars, all of whom had to be sent home, wherefrom they never returned. Were I a believer in judgments or reprisals, I should certainly set this down as belonging thereto. The consequence was that "Othello's occupation was gone," and I had to seek for " fresh fields and pastures new."

The 5th of November was, at Uxbridge, at this period, as in most other towns, kept up with great spirit. The chief pyrotechnist of the town was a person named Norwood, who also managed the spinning business for Mrs. Redford, for whom my master worked. The large trade done by Norwood excited the envy of my employer, and he accordingly started firework making. In this new business I was called on to assist. My position was an unfortunate one, insofar as I had started a sort of an agency for the fireworks of Norwood's manufacture, and it is more than possible that my accounts of the sale I had effected gave spur to the opposition. At any rate, the start was made, and, sworn to secrecy, we set to work in a business of which it was subsequently proved we knew little or nothing. When we had prepared a sufficient quantity, my master insisted that I should sell his fireworks and his only; but upon reflection he decided that I might sell both. In order to beat Norwood out of the market, my master had determined to make his squibs double the size of those he wished to supplant. In accordance with instructions given, I was, in all instances, to force the sale of the wares of my employer. This I did, but purchasers soon discovered that size does not ensure quality, and the result was that they refused to purchase our "Woolwich infants." I am bound to confess that they had good grounds for their preference, for, while Norwood's deminutive squibs, when lighted, flew about in all directions and finished with a report as loud as that of an ordinary musket, our own exhibited a pitiful amount of laziness and ended as often without a bang as with one. As I was going to my work one morning I was met by Mr. Norwood and charged with representing Matthews' fireworks as those of his make. The charge was perfectly true, and I admitted it ; but I excused myself upon the ground that I had been instructed to do so by my master. I was old enough to know that I was playing a disgraceful part, and also to despise the man who prompted me ; but I valued my place, insofar as it enabled me to contribute to a poverty-stricken home that could ill afford to lose my trifling earnings. Simple as this incident may appear, it taught me the necessity of distinguishing between profession and practice. Had you taken my employer at his word, or judged by his outward life, you would have deemed it an impossibility that he could have advised the evil act just described. I have over and over again blamed myself for becoming his dupe or agent, but then I have found some sort of consolation in the fact that I was not more than twelve years of age, and that I was largely instigated by my desire to retain my place in the interests of my parents, brothers, and sisters. It became clear to me, if not at the time, by subsequent reflection, that a constant attendance at church or chapel, and a mere profession of religion, form no criterion whatever of the man, and a pretty large admixture with doubters and believers has proved to me that, of the two, I would rather trust the former. "The paucity of Christians," Leigh Hunt said, "is astonishing, considering the number of them !"

I remained under the rope-spinner some twelve months or more, and then succeeded a friend as rural post boy. This was under the post master of Uxbridge, William Lake, a printer and stationer. It was then the custom to charge a penny over and above the ordinary post office charge for the delivery of each letter beyond the town paving. This additional sum went to swell the post master's salary, whatever that might have been, less the cost of wages paid to those engaged in the delivery. The portion of country allotted to me consisted of Uxbridge Common, Ickenham, Ruislip, Eastcote, and their outlyings. I usually reached the office not later than six o'clock, winter and summer. The farthest point of my round may be taken to have been seven miles from the office; but my day's journey, out and home, could not have averaged much less than from sixteen to twenty miles. I usually arrived home about dinner time, and the remainder of my time was spent at presswork. At that period, Sunday delivery was in vogue. For this amount of labour, I was paid the munificent sum of three shillings per week.

The duties for one so young were undoubtedly severe, and the pay ridiculously small; but I was pleased with the appointment. My daily round was through pleasant fields, where birds sang and flowers grew. I saw the squirrel leap from tree to tree, wild rabbits sporting, the partridge whirring from my feet, the mowers and reapers at their labours, and, better still, I was welcomed wherever I went. It was something to have a letter in those days. It was the talk of the villagers. "Got any there for me, postman?" persons would ask, who never had had a letter in their lives, and turn away desparingly as I answered, "No." Then there were occasions when I was called upon to read their contents, and I found I had power to create smiles and draw forth tears. I was a boy and the listeners adult personages. I could do what they could not—they were dependent on me. I liked reading letters, and I did read them for there were no envelopes in those days to prevent me doing so. I was in the possession of secret knowledge, and like a crafty statesman, I was proud of it.

After being thus engaged for a twelvemonth, I had become so useful in the printing office in my spare time that the foreman interceded with the master to get me apprenticed, and in this he succeeded. My education was miserably deficient for such an occupation, and my first proof occasioned roars of laughter. Still, it was my mother's education, and was not to be judged by its earlier fruits. Three years passed, and despite of my ambition to become a scholar and master of my trade, I had made little or no progress.

It would weary my readers' patience to describe fully the incidents of my early life; I will, therefore, be content to deal with those that recall the most pleasant memories. When not otherwise profitably engaged, it was customary, at the close of the harvest, to be drifted to the cornfields. At sunrise we would leave home, the place and time for meeting being arranged on the night previous. The company consisted chiefly of lads and lasses, with a sprinkling of grown up persons. After breakfast, it was our custom to toil on till near noon when we would gather in the shade of a neighbouring tree. This was called "bever" time, and the meal was looked upon as the most important of the day. Having a pleasant voice, and carrying with me a goodly budget of ditties, it became the custom at its close to invite me to lead off with a song. It was useless to refuse. Indeed, who ever did refuse, dear old mother Hitchings? This gander of the flock, backed by her known kindness, her weather worn cheeks and black piercing eyes, was irresistible. She had marched through the battle fields of the Peninsula with Wellington, and had gleaned them after Death's harvest. She was one whom war had not robbed of a generous heart.

Few of the present generation know aught respecting the old tinder box and matches. They have never heard the damp tinder cursed, the clic clic of the flint against the steel and the steady action of the human breath to encourage the tiny spark to spread. Many are doubtless yet impressed with the belief that just as we get a light to day from a simple scratch, so their ancestors got it before them. Why should I introduce matches? simply because the first light I ever saw struck outside a tinder box was by this very woman. We were gleaning on the same furrow together, when all of a sudden, she ceased, and diving her hand into her pocket brought forth a box. Placing a small piece of card between two other pieces, or rather one piece bent, she drew the former sharply forth, and there was fire—fire that lit her pipe, and that would moreover have destroyed London, just as Pompeii perished from a cinder. If ever I stared in astonishment, it was then. I had heard of witches, and verily I thought Mrs. Hitchings none other. I have seen many gleaners : but never one to equal this woman. She was not a straight-backed one, not a gleaner with one hand only. Left and right, she nipped up the scattered ears, and when night came you would see her marching under a bundle, that, for size and weight, put all others in the shade. Ailments she appeared to have none. Bronzed face, square of build, good tempered—rough or smooth, there stood a woman with a man's courage and a man's strength and endurance. Many, sick and wounded, I warrant had had in times past good cause to bless her, and if she did filch a trifle from their pockets when dead, she earned it, I warrant, by her readiness to assist and comfort them while living.

The custom of gleaning I am told is fast vanishing. On many farms it is not permitted, the old scriptural behoof being forgotten, perhaps from the fact that more persons can read the bible now than formerly. But then they have no occasion to halt and spell the words like those who preceded them, and so fail to be impressed with their teaching. Who knows the meaning of a "grist" mill now-a-days? Take a bushel of corn to one, and ten chances to one but what you would be charged for grinding the same. If ever I was happy, it was in the gleaning or, as more often called in that part of the country, "leasing" field.

The company of leasers usually consisted of boys and girls—old enough to have their fancies, and feel the pangs of jealousy. Breakfast in the field before starting to labour. Bever as before described. Dinner, if we had any ; if not content till we reached home at seven or eight in the evening. Then, gleaning over, we hammered out the corn with a cudgel, to separate the grain from the chaff, tossed it from a plate, leaving the wind to do the rest, having previously spread a sheet to prevent waste.

I have failed to do justice to old Tom Sutton, or rather "Uncle Tom," as we used to call him. What a merry man he might have been and what a miserable man he was, or rather I ought to describe him as miserable as a man of his nature could be. His wife, my maternal aunt, descended the gamut of religions sectaries, beginning with the church of England and ending as near the "Muggletonians" as age would permit. She would rather "reign in hell than serve in heaven," and yet, with all her faults, I feel sure that she was impressed that she was only doing her duty, and contributing to the happiness of those around her. She was the bell-weather of the Stanwell Moor flock, and no matter whatever new sect she joined, others were sure to follow. In her latter days, having exhausted the religions that had gained a footing on the swampy dependency of the village of Stanwell, she joined a chapel in Staines, some two miles distant, and thither she would trudge on each successive Sunday morning, carrying with her cold food sufficient for the day. The Sabbath was the one day in the week poor Tom could call his own, and to be lugged off, wet or dry, on that day, to hear sermons preached that he did not understand and to be fed on stale sandwiches, was not cheering. Whether this treatment made him a saint, I do not pretend to determine.

When I was a boy, I was as daring as most boys are, and, on more than one occasion, was nearly paying a heavy fine for my folly. I was very proud of being able to grasp the limb of a tree, and thereby hang on, with my legs, head downwards, my hands being free to clap at my own supposed cleverness. One holiday afternoon, on attempting this feat from a limb of a tall elm, I did not heed that it rose almost parallel with the trunk. The result was that when I desired to recover myself from my position, I failed to raise the uppermost part of my body high enough to reach the branch from which I was hanging. I tried again and again, and on each occasion, failed. I was nearly spent with these successive efforts. I cast my eyes to the earth and was horror-stricken at the depth I imagined I should have to fall. In my despair, I made a supernatural effort, and, fortunately succeeded in clutching the limb. Had I failed in this despairing effort, I must have fallen with fatal consequences. I remember how, with a sensation of fever running through me, I in haste descended, thankful for my escape, and vowing I would never attempt the feat again. I never passed that tree without feeling a cold shudder running through me.

On another occasion, in order to save the reputation of a quondam lover, I climbed a stable-roof in order to escape from a cul-de-sac. It was pitch dark, but by the aid of a ladder, I manged to get on to the roof. After crawling to its topmost ridge, at the risk of rolling on the other side, I peered over, but it was too dark to see what was below. There was only one alternative to allowing myself to roll off, and that was to go back. This I determined not to do, and shouting, "Here goes!" I made the venture, to find that I had landed on the backs of a sow and her litter of young pigs! The horrid and terrified yells of the mother and her young were fearful, and, solely to my nimbleness, I doubtlessly owed my escape.

At this period Uxbridge was favourable to the drama, and was visited by Jackson's Company. It is now greatly changed in this respect. This change is doubtlessly due to many causes, the chief being the easy communication that the town now enjoys with the metropolis. Despite of my youth, through the assistance rendered by a friend, I managed to become associated with several of the actors, and I confess I was proud of the acquaintance thus formed. Among others, I became friendly with the famous Frederick Robson, who then occupied the position of second low comedian, an actor named Tommy Styles being the first. I have good grounds for saying that at this time Robson's salary only amounted to fifteen shillings per week and a benefit. But it was a benefit, not in name; but in eality. With his songs between the acts, he carried everything before him. His chances of displaying his powers as an actor were exceedingly few; but, few as they were, I felt assured that he had marvellous powers and only wanted the opportunity to ensure their recognition. In this I was not deceived. He became, as all the world knows, the greatest living actor of his time, in the path he had chosen; indeed when I recall to my remembrance his Simon Burr, his Macbeth, his Yellow Dwarf, his Medea, and a score of other parts, I doubt if he was ever equalled. Remembering our close friendship during his stay in my native town, I could not help thinking, as I saw him alight from his Brougham at the Olympic, that I would have given the world to have reminded him of our former intimacy, and many a time, as I stood watching him alight, did I endeavour to summon up resolution; but all to no purpose. The thought would come that I might possibly get snubbed for my pains. At that time, I had a burlesque half written, and I was vain enough to imagine that I had only to get him to peruse it to secure its being acted. But, with the copy in my hand, after declaring "it shall be done," each resolution would vanish ere I could carry it out. That burlesque, or rather the written portion thereof, after being lost and found at least a dozen times, disappeared for ever, and as I have long come to the conclusion that burlesque has had a most injurious influence upon the national character, I am rather pleased than otherwise. I know its influence on myself. During the past twenty years, it mattered not what circle you moved in, it was more or less contaminated with its vicious influence. So long as a laugh was raised, it mattered not at whose expense, or at what cost. Our greatest and most sacred authors and their purest thoughts, were turned into ridicule. That I had a tendency to follow this evil habit is to me a source of regret. From what I have since learned of my friend, Robson, I have every reason to believe that, had I made myself known to him, I should have met with a cordial reception.

About this time a Mr. Woolridge visited the town in the capacity of manager of a travelling theatre. The result was utter failure, and had it not been for the conception of a happy thought, ruin must have ensued. In their difficulties the proprietor and members attended the "Falcon Free and Easy" of which I was the permanent chairman. After contributing largely to the Company's amusement, one of them claimed my attention. This was willingly accorded, and forthwith he narrated the history of their difficulties.

This so excited the sympathy of those present, that they offered to do all in their power to assist them. After a while, it was agreed that the best plan would be an amateur performance. The play chosen was "The Fire Raiser;" or "Roundheads and Cavaliers," in which I played the part of Piers Talbot, and three friends of my own, characters of minor importance. For this entertainment I undertook to supply the bills. It was not long before these were issued, and as the announcement thus made afforded no clue to the personality of the actors; naturally a deal of curiosity was excited. This curiosity was increased considerably by rumours cunningly devised that they were, persons of the highest social position. The result was that when the theatre doors were thrown open, the accommodation was inadequate to hold half the persons seeking admission. Three of the four "gentlemen," save the mark, for we were only four ill-paid apprentices, kept their word, and arrived at the theatre at the appointed time. In order that the secret should remain intact till we reached the theatre, a considerable detour was made. There was no rehearsal, and as neither of the three persons alluded to had previously spoken a line, on or off the boards of a theatre, it may readily be expected that all did not go smoothly. As Piers Talbot, I wore a green velvet tunic, a lace collar, a pair of white trousers, and a paper head-dress, adorned with peacock's feathers. In fact, my appearance was that of a Sherwood forester, less the bow and quiver. The velvet of the tunic it is true, was considerably worn and a vast number of the spangles were conspicuous by their absence. My make-up, bad as it was, brought down a round of applause. I had not proceeded far in my introductory speech, commencing "After a tedious absence, welcome my native land," when my attention was directed to a pair of youths who had been stowed away in the orchestra, disputing in regard to my identity, one offering to stake a penny that I was Jack Leno, and the other offering to bet a mint of money

I was not a bit like him. With every disadvantage, we managed to pull through, after which the company played the "Dead Shot," which so pleased the audience that, after a stay of over nine months, the manager left the town with sufficient money to restock the theatre with entirely new scenery and a wardrobe of which the proprietor of any "fix up" might well be proud.

I learned from a book written by my friend Mr. Charles Hindley that Woolridge realised a large fortune in Australia, and I am pleased to know that he attributed his success mainly to our joint efforts to assist him out of his difficulties.

The fires in country towns like Uxbridge are things of rare occurrence, and in consequence, are matters often remembered. On the 22nd day of April, 1839, I well remember my father entering the room in which I and my brothers slept. I likewise remember hearing him open the window, and also the following between him, and one Smith, a miller, who lived next door. "I believe John," said the latter, "it is those two hayricks in Pen Fields."

"No," replied my father, "If I am not greatly mistaken, it is your mill that is on fire, and so they ultimately agreed.

"May I come? father,"

"No, certainly not," was the reply.

I stood watching the fire, the temptation to be present was too great, and I eventually could resist it no longer. I soon reached the scene of the fire, and although some hours had elapsed since my attention had been called to it, it was in full blaze on my arrival. Of course, seeing the people busy, I was desirous of assisting, and speedily armed myself with a leather pail, and finding the water running freely from the mill-head, I jumped on to a plank stretched across the same, and dipped my bucket into the stream. It was instantly filled and drawn under the plank. I held on with all my might, but it pulled too forcibly for my then strength. Still, I held on, and should have undoubtedly been pulled into the current, if the handle of the vessel had not given way. On seeing the bucket floating away, I was terribly frightened, thinking I had been guilty of a great crime. Finding I was unobserved, I threw the handle after the pail, and made for home. The mill and its contents were destroyed. For many years after the mantel shelves of the poor were ornamented with curious relics of the fire.

The fire at Hillingdon or Rockingham House, it having formerly been the mansion of the premier, Rockingham, broke out on Sunday, February 4, 1844. As it was the only other notable fire in Uxbridge that I remember to have taken part in, it will be as well if I mention it here, instead of in its chronological order. On the Sunday morning in question, a friend and I were taking our usual rest-day walk, when we saw flames in the direction of, and, as it proved, from the mansion named. To these, we called the attention of West, who was employed on the estate, and a dweller on its border. He at once was satisfied from whence the flames proceeded, let us pass through his garden which led to the park, and accompanied us to the scene of the disaster. When we reached the mansion, its inmates had only just become acquainted with the accident. The news quickly spread. the service in both Uxbridge and Hillingdon church was ended, and, in a short time, the town engine arrived, with a crowd of followers. By the time it arrived, however, those early on the spot were busily engaged within its walls removing the furniture and valuable contents. Suddenly, we heard shouts of danger, and these not a moment too soon, for in fact, I and a few others were imprisoned by the flames. We dashed through them at full speed. and, as we left the building, its roof fell with a crash. Happily, the warning had been heard by all within the building, and obeyed.

I could willingly and pleasantly linger on the life I led up till the hour of my apprenticeship, but the exigency of space debars me from the pleasure it would not fail to give me. This life did not differ materially from that of the majority of those of youths in a similar station to myself. The task of recording its most important incidents would not be great, for, despite of having never made a note, even the most trivial incidents remain firmly embedded in my memory, while matters of greater importance of yesterday's occurrence, are partly or totally obliterated. Inasmuch, however, as the readers of my poems are already acquainted with the most striking events, their absence will not be either missed or deplored.

I know not how it occurred, but by far the cleverest man in the office, a Mr. Kingsbury, conceived a great liking for me, and, at his invitation, I stayed at the office beyond the usual hours, in order that I might benefit by his instruction It has been my lot to become acquainted with many wonderful men in my time ; but I owe it to the memory of my first benefactor, to say that I never yet met with his equal for general intelligence and all round ability. However he could have had the courage to persevere with a scholar like me has always been a mystery. Possibly he saw that I had the will, and estimated that important factor at its true value.

Then, my half hours schooling over, I used to accompany him to the "Dolphin," on the Moor, where it was his custom to give me one half pint of ale. If interested by the conversation, I by chance dawdled over the drinking of the said half pint, I was quietly reminded that my time had expired.

One evening at the office, I was more than usually low-spirited, so much so that my condition attracted my friend's attention. I confessed that it was caused by my inability to learn my trade and profit by his instructions. For a long time I was impervious to all he said by way of encouragement, and shed tears plentifully. At length, however, he so far succeeded in inspiring me with fresh hope, that I promised I would never give way to despair again, and I kept my word, at least, till I was well out of the difficulties that then weighed me down. I have lived long enough to know that tears are not always a sign of defeat. From that hour light seemed to break in upon me, and it is more than probable that I had been passing through the stupid period of my existence, in other words that physical and other changes were taking place that rendered mental progress impossible. In truth, I grew so fast that I converted my trousers into breeches ; or, in other words, what would now be called, knickerbockers.

During the early portion of my apprenticeship, my father's

uncle, Matthew Leno, of Staines, Middlesex, died. In the last government lottery, he had the good fortune to hold the ticket for the grand prize. With this, he left the "Chequers" at Fly's Wash, a wayside house between Redbourne and Markyate Street, Herts, to lead a retired life at the place named. At his death, my father acquired a small portion of his fortune, and, with it, opened a new house, devoted to the sale of malt liquors. A sense of shame and disgust comes over me whenever I refer back to this period of my life, and remember how my father was systematically fleeced, and how I used to be called on to amuse the fleecers, by my singing. I remember how I used to be pitted against the son of a drunken customer, and how we used to struggle for mastery, like a pair of piping bullfinches, and how, as I imagine, to please my father, the palm of victory used to be awarded to me. Still, when I remember the foaming pots of ale that were placed on the table free of payment, and the long scores that were never liquidated, I have my suspicion that the award was not, in all instances, fairly made. Thus the money my father made through his uncle's will was soon exhausted, and, slowly but surely, we drifted back to our old quarters. It was while living at the "Rising Sun," that Fred Farrell first came to reside with us, and with him a Welshman named Jenkins, both members of the "gentle craft." But, in this instance, birds of a feather did not flock together. Jenkins was a rogue; Farrell one of the best men that ever breathed. Jenkins left us greatly in debt. On his departure, it was discovered that he had left a box behind. This was securely fastened, and, on it, was placed a note saying the box and contents would be redeemed speedily. After waiting a considerable period for the remittance, the box was forced, and found to contain a vast quantity of brickbats and an odd volume of Johnson's "Lives of the Poets." The poring over of that volume possibly helped to decide that I should turn versifier.

My friends, Kingsbury and Farrell, though both Liberals, were of different schools of liberalism. Kingsbury, a Free Trader and follower of Richard Cobden, and Farrell a Chartist, and something more—a devoted follower of O'Connor and Robert Owen, and a great admirer of Richard Oastler, the so-called "Factory King." As Kingsbury and Farrell lost no opportunity of advancing their views, I was soon possessed of a tolerable knowledge of the tenets of each. This was supplemented by the perusal of the tracts issued by the Anti-Corn-law League, and the "Examiner" newspaper. Farrell lent me the former, the "Star," and the "New Moral World," and his opponent their antidotes. What my own opinions were at this time, it would be somewhat difficult to determine. All I remember is that I soon began to dispute with my masters, and that I availed myself freely of Farrell's arguments to demolish those of Kingsbury, and of those of the latter to upset those advanced by Farrell, and of both, to demolish any stray antagonist. In the end my allegiance went with the Chartists, and with them, I opposed the Free Trade of Cobden and Bright. It is a mistake to suppose that the Chartists were in favour of protective duties on corn, or that they had the least sympathy with landlord Protection. Their doctrine was Free Trade in corn, raw materials of all kinds, and in all articles of foreign growth and manufacture that did not run counter to English produce. They were in favour of protective duties on silk manufactures, watches, and, indeed, all manufactured articles that needed protection. In fact, they were believers in neither Free Trade or Protection, wholly and solely, but in an ajustment of both. Whether they were right or wrong, I will not stay to argue. All I can say is that I have, for many years, been a Free-trader.

At the earliest opportunity, I joined the Chartist Movement, by taking up my card, and I soon afterwards succeded in forming a branch thereof in my native town, to which I acted as secretary. As far as my means would allow, I contributed to the cheaper publications devoted to the advocacy of the Charter, and, moreover, undertook the sale thereof. These papers I obtained from a travelling retail newsman, whose weekly round embraced Uxbridge, although his starting point was the metropolis. As I had no allowance of profit, and a few of my customers forgot to pay, I speedily found that the loss occasioned, was more than I could bear, in fact that the small amount that I was allowed for pocket money was more than swallowed up. Still, by knocking off the defaulters, I managed to continue to act as a distributor till these ephemeral publications ceased to appear.

The Falcon Harmonic Meetings were models of their kind. I had it pretty much my own way, despite my extreme youth. Songs, popularly known as "blue," were then in fashion, but I succeeded, after a deal of opposition, in banishing them from the entertainment, and had the satisfaction in after years of receiving the thanks of several of my bitterest opponents. "If you cannot be witty without being filthy," I was wont to say, "your presence is not required here." I successfully instituted the practice of setting aside certain evenings for the songs of certain writers, and on these anniversaries, would usually commence the proceedings with a short biographical and critical lecture on the song writers whose songs were intended to follow. All such announcements were made in advance, and arrangements made with the singers who frequented the room, with regard to the songs to be sung. It often occurred that the songs thus specially provided for would not last out the evening, but the difficulty was easily got over by winding up with others. There is one incident connected with these free and easies that I desire to tell. On my farewell night, after occupying the post of honour at least three successive years, it was arranged that I should repeat my lecture on Burns, indeed, that we should have a Burns' night. It so happened that a retired Scotch physician, who had settled in the town, chanced to read this notice, and, interested in all related to his gifted countryman, timidly asked the landlady if he would be allowed admission. She referred him to me, and I at once told him that there was nothing to prevent his presence, as indeed there was not. He stayed till the last. It was my usual custom by way of closing the entertainment to sing an impromptu song. Feeling somewhat proud of the stranger's presence, I invited him to give a subject. In compliance he gave "War." I have ceased to have much belief in impromptu songs, they are poor rubbish, at the best. Nevertheless the old gentleman was so pleased with my effort, that I was asked if I could give him a copy. No sooner had I done so, the words were possibly considerably improved in the reproduction, than he had them printed, and for days afterwards, he might have been seen in the loitering shops of the town, of which Lake's was one, pointing them out as something truly wonderful. At the close of the proceedings, the old gentleman expressed his delight at the entertainment, and hearing that I was about leaving the town in search of employment, promised if in want, and I would only write to him, he would at once render me assistance. He had known Burns personally.

The house was kept by a young widow, left with two children. At this period it was generally believed that my old friend, Stephen Capp, was about to marry her. Such doubtless was his intention, but he so dallied over the affair, that she, tired of waiting, got married to another. At this Stephen flew off to Australia, and there ended a life which had been up to this disappointment, characterised by sober, plodding industry, and habits of providence, in sottish inactivity and absolute poverty. This change was the more remarkable from the fact that Steve was considerably advanced in years, and, as was generally thought, of fixed habits. It was about this period that Mike, the dwarf waiter, fell ill. His mistress and others of her family being worn out by watching, the landlady appealed to me to take a turn. I at once consented, and the widow much pleased sat about mixing me grog for the night. I asked to be allowed to glance over her library, and, from its contents, I selected "Young's Night Thoughts." This I managed to finish before morning, and never was book read to greater advantage. The moans, occasional ravings and wanderings of my poor little friend and former schoolfellow enabled me to realise beauties that I had failed to see in a previous perusal. How much a book gains by the appropriate surroundings of the person reading it, was forcibly impressed upon me, and this fact was farther corroborated years after, when I read Scott's "Lady of the Lake," during a walk from the Trosachs to Stirling. The enormous popularity that Young's now greatly neglected poem once enjoyed is shown by the numerous quotations that linger in our memories, "familiar as household words."

I was born in the P season and, strangely enough, have been Pieman, Pastrycook, Printer, Publisher, Politician and Poetaster. It so occurred that, in order to meet the demand for pies for the coming Saturday, we had made an unusually large quantity. On that day my father was engaged to wait at a gentleman's residence, a business he could not afford to neglect. While at dinner on Saturday, my poor mother began a doleful story of the great loss that would ensue from the pies being left unsold. I could see clearly that she was indirectly asking me to return and sell the pies. Candidly, it was a job not to my liking. I was getting towards the end of my apprenticeship, and was looked upon as holding a highly respectable position. My companions were socially far more highly placed than myself. It was a question of pride versus duty. I am proud to say that duty won. "Give me father's apron," I said on returning from the printing office, and, donning it, I marched into the High Street, with the pie-tin, shouting, "Toss or buy, hot pies!" &c.. I found it like bathing. When I was in, I rather liked it, though I had shivered on the bank. It was such a novelty to see me playing the part of pieman, that customers came, thick and fast, and, within an hour at the utmost, I had sold out, or tossed out, finding myself a winner to the extent of a shilling or two. My poor mother's blessings were by no means rare; but, I verily believe I never received such blessings as I did on the evening in question. I would that I could now see the smile that lit her face, as she returned to me my winnings, or "over money," as father used to call them. It may appear ridiculous in the eyes of my readers; but there is no action of my life of which I feel prouder. If there should be any doubt about my right to entertain this opinion, ask a particular friend to sweep a crossing for your especial benefit, and mark the answer. But, stay! am I not equally proud of my singing a song for the old tramp from Hitching to earn him a bed? I will not attempt to decide which was the better act. I am pleased to be proud of both of them.

My apprenticeship was drawing to a close. Despite of my ability to seek and find enjoyment, those seven years seemed terribly long. Through a quarrel with my father, I left home ere it had half expired, and found shelter with my grandmother. How I contrived to live on the sums of four shillings and sixpence, and five shillings per week, and yet be able to visit the "Falcon," will puzzle my readers. Well, the truth is, I became an expert gambler. Not a cheat, but an expert. There was not a game that I played at that I did not make myself master of. I did not hide my ability; it was known and admitted. I knew my own powers, and backed myself. Occasionally I made miscalculations and got broke; but as the men in the office gloried in my cleverness, I was not at a loss for the wherewithal for a fresh start. There was never a day but what I was asked to recount my victories. If, in return, I had to recount a defeat, I was generally consoled with an expressed belief that I would soon find my revenge and a query as to how much I wanted to borrow. My winnings at least provided me with pocket money, and I contrived to live on my wages, miserable as they undoubtedly were. A penny rasher and a few potatoes furnished me with a dinner, two-penny worth of bread and cheese with a supper, and, as for breakfast and tea, these were meals that I never cared much for, and they were in no sense expensive. I had rent free, and my washing cost me nothing. And yet, despite of the meanness of my living, I was both hearty and strong. This proves to me that it does not require a deal to support a healthy frame, providing that the little eaten be taken at regular intervals. It is one thing to put food into your stomach, and another to be able to extract every particle of support from it.

I had fully expected that my apprenticeship finished, I should continue in the employment of my master as a journeyman, but in this I was doomed to be mistaken. Unfortunately for me my master was on the verge of bankruptcy, and, in his difficulties, had borrowed money from a person who although a journeyman, was my inferior in the office. The first intimation I had of this was a command from my master to hand over the books of office accounts to this person. As I had fairly won my position as foreman, though only an apprentice, and, knowingly had done nothing to lessen confidence in me, I naturally asked for an explanation. This was refused with the intimation that it would be revealed later on. I soon had reason to suspect the true cause, the clue being revealed by the extraordinary liberties taken by the person in question. I had the satisfaction of knowing that he was cordially hated by all engaged on the premises, and that my treatment was looked upon as harsh and unmerited. Among the liberties to which I refer, was the firing off a gun from the office window, in the garden, and elsewhere in office hours. One day he called my attention, to a blackbird seated on an apple tree in a straight line to which was a gentleman's house. "If I fire," said he, raising his gun, "will the shots harm the glass?" I ridiculed the idea, being fully impressed with what would follow. "Bang" went the gun, and there was work for the glazier. That ended the shooting at least for some time. The exact cost of repairing I do not remember, I know I was to blame; but who is there who would not have felt pleased, as I confessedly did, under the circumstances?

My master was too much in this person's debt to punish this offence as it deserved. When I had "picked up my last stick" as an apprentice, "I asked if my services would be required, and as I had learned to expect was told no. A Mr. Haddock was, however, finessing for the business in the event of the looming brankruptcy being fatal to the prospects of my old master, and on my telling him I was about to leave the town in search of work, he invited me to stay, promising me the management of the printing department in the event of his success. In this he was disappointed, and eventually I was forced to leave in search of work. I thought I should like to try the West, the worst quarter I could possibly have selected, judged by the doctrine of chances. I had not a penny piece, mother had sixpence. This she gave me supplemented with her blessings and tears. I thought, ere leaving the town, I would call on an old friend, William Austin, who kept a small proprietary school. I told him my intention. He pressed me to put my resolution off till the morrow, saying that I would confer a great favour on him if I would take charge of his school for a few hours. I consented, to delay my starting, in order that he might meet his daughter; but told him I still adhered to my determination to quit the town that day. With this understanding, he left, and punctually returned at the time promised. It was true, as he argued, that to my chances a day was of not much consequence, but I could not face the ordeal of a second parting with my broken-hearted mother. He was as poor as myself; but he must needs give me something; it was an uncut seed cake, a present from his motherless daughter, and of her own making, in the interval. This I refused to take; but he chided me for my folly, attributed it to pride, and ultimately I consented. As you leave Uxbridge by the Windsor Road, a steep hill has to be climbed. From its top you catch a capital bird's eye view of the old town. There it lies at your feet, the most conspicuous objects being the tower of the church and the market house. On reaching the top of the hill, I turned round, knowing that a few steps onward the old town would be hidden from my sight. I shall never forget the feeling that came over me as I turned and gazed on that storehouse of pleasant memories. I was leaving everything I had learned to prize, every friend I had. Every remembrance worth cherishing lie centred there; it had been my world; it was my world. I tore myself from it with a sudden wrench, preferring a sharp pang to a lingering pain. I took my hat from my head, tossed it in the air, caught it, clapped it on my head, and, mindful of the fate of Lot's wife, turned and never looked back. I reached Eton, got work at the College office, gave my seed cake to a cripple, and arrived back the same evening to turn my mother's sorrow into joy, and cheat a few of my old friends into the belief that I had turned coward and retreated!

During my apprenticeship, a cry of "help" was heard issuing from the house of Captain Harris. Looking from the window, I thought I saw a woman bleeding, I immediately announced my intention of jumping from the window, in order to render assistance. Fearless of danger, I leaped on to the closet below and from its roof into the garden. Two ladies belonging to the garden, seeing I was making for the garden wall, threw open the door in the garden boundary and directed my attention to it. I darted through the opening, and made for the Captain's residence. On reaching it, I saw a burly man in the front parlour, armed with a thick cudgel. It so occurred that some builders at work on the premises had left a plank agains' the window by the help of which the thief had gained admittance. Availing myself of this, I, despite his threatening attitude, ascended. On seeing me, he let fall his booty, and I seized him by the collar of his coat, and so held him, till the police arrived. Others who had rendered me assistance, claimed the credit of the capture, and the result was that I gave up all claim to the honour in disgust. The unfortunate lady of the house had been seriously injured, and died a few months afterwards. The robber was convicted, but I fail to remember the sentence passed upon him.

There is one incident connected with my stay at Eton that I cannot forebear relating. One day, as I was passing through the front shop on my way to the printing office, a scholar took the liberty of cramming a snowball down my neck. For this I demanded an apology, which he refused to give. I politely told him the consequence likely to result for his persistency in refusing to apologise. This had no affect, and in a moment I floored him. I of course thought my discharge would follow, but, to my agreeable surprise, I got complimented by the head shopman, who was witness to the entire affair, and who had been a martyr to the continuous insults of the offender and his associates.

While at Eton, I managed to convert the whole of the printers, with the exception of the foreman, to my way of thinking. In argument, he was decidedly my inferior, and just as I succeeded in turning the laugh against him, I played ducks and drakes with the tenure of my position. At the end of twelve months I was told by the foreman that work had run out, and I must accept of the usual notice. This I knew to be false. I consulted my friends, and the result was that I determined to seek Mr. Williams, and thank him for favours received. He was astonished to hear that I was about leaving, inquired the cause, and, on being told, scarcity of work, pooh-poohed the idea, told me it was a mistake, and told me to come on the following Monday, as usual. On entering the printing office, the foreman asked me if I had left anything behind? I said I had not; but I had come back to renew my labours at the bidding of the master. He said that he had no work to give me. To this, I was in a position to give him a direct denial by drawing his attention to the fact that he had copy for a new work in his drawer, which had remained untouched for over two months, although the work was much wanted. At this, my friends sat up a perfect roar of laughter, which I could have very well spared. The truth was they gloried in seeing Tommy Hughes beaten, and in my return, for I was a general favourite. On a second discharge from the foreman, I successfully played the trick over again, and I verily believe the foreman would have cut my throat had he dared. On attempting it a third time, I found the cause assigned a valid one. Still with all the antagonism that raged between us, I attribute little blame to Thomas Hughes. There were faults on both sides. I had no right to break down his authority, and he, being the older and more experienced, should have refused to discuss political matters with me in office hours. I was earnest in my views and naturally desirous of making proselytes. Indeed I lost no opportunity, fearless of the consequences to myself. It was customary to bow to Mr. Williams wherever met. To this I demurred, and the rest followed suit. The change did not escape his notice, and meeting myself and others he saluted us. "Now lads," said I, "you may bow as long and as low as you like. Master and man I always thought were on an equality—outside the workshop. They are naturally dependent on each other, and there is no valid reason why the latter should cringe to the former. One sells and the other buys labour. As a master, I wanted no subserviency; save that which I had a right to expect, and as a workman I refused to acknowledge any indebtedness or inferiority. Had I received more for my labour than it was worth, I might have thought differently. Perhaps my most serious offence was my starting in the royal town of Windsor a branch of the Chartist organization. Not to dwell on this portion of my history, when I did leave, I had the satisfaction of being told by Mr. Williams, that if I referred to him, I need not fear the character he was prepared to give me, and that if I determined to go to London, I might use his name with a printer with whom he was on friendly terms. Of the result I shall have occasion to speak further on. My singing qualities stood me in good stead, although on one occasion they were nigh getting me into trouble. I had written a song against the use of the lash. This song became exceedingly popular with the civilian portion of the public. Strange to say it was taken exception to by a sergeant and a corporal of the Blues. In consequence of my determination to sing it when and whenever I pleased, they entered the room with several friends, and under the influence of liquor, vented their spite on the company, the chairs and tables and the landlord. Fortunately for me, I was not present, or the poker that smashed the counter might have come in contact with my head. We had determined to march to London on the 10th of April, 1848, but when we read the letter of Fergus O'Conner resisting all idea of resisting the authorities, we looked upon this as an act of cowardice, and determined to take no part in what we deemed to be a farce. In those days, I believed more in fighting than I do now. In truth I was for rebellion and civil war, and despaired of ever obtaining justice, or what I then conceived it to be, save by revolution. While bitterly opposed to aught savouring of physical force now ; I still hold that given certain conditions, its use is fully justifiable, the fact being that those who condemn its use in favour of right, seldom object to its use when wrong is to be conserved. We have the examples of America, of France, of Italy, of England before us, to confute those who declare that nothing is to be done by force. The Freedom of America, of France, of Italy, and indeed of England, is directly traceable to it. In a nation where, as in England today, the force of public opinion is allowed to prevail, it is a crime to dream of resorting to civil war; but in nations where tyranny prevails and every attempt to obtain right is met with imprisonment, rebellion and war are justified, so soon as there is a fair prospect of their proving successful. What but a determination to fight gave the barons victory over John, the Commonwealth over the King, of the middle class reformers of 1832, over the court and the privileged few? I confess that since the people are more fairly represented and legal means are provided to introduce measures of reform, that conspiracy, or the use of armed force, is a crime of the greatest magnitude, and assuredly one to which I would be, on no consideration, a party. It is in the conditions rather than myself that the change must be sought. Forcibly withdraw the rights that have been won, illegally attempt to infringe and overthrow the right of thought and of speech, and I cease to preach peace and forbearance, or retain my faith on the awakening of the wrong doer to the evil of his ways. The crime, if crime it be, would not be of my seeking, nor of those with me, but of those guilty of arrogating to themselves a power of life and death over those they had defrauded of their birthrights. Let the exceptions here pointed to be recognised. I am not one of those who, smitten on the right cheek would turn the left to the striker. Upon the contrary, if wrongly struck, I will return the blow whenever a fair chance of punishment to the evil-doer presents itself. To do otherwise, would be to court slavery, and what is more, deserve it. Neither the rights of this or any other nation were won by such arrant cowardice.

With my home life, I am not desirous of dealing. The fact is that it would fail to prove interesting to strangers, and it was with no conception that it would that I commenced this autobiography. I got mated young, too young many would say, but, for my part, I do not regret it. My partner was ten years older than myself, and this I hold to have been an advantage. Our union lasted for forty years, and the fruits thereof consisted of two male and four female children who grew up to puberty, and of whom four females and one male are yet living. To say that we never quarrelled would be an untruth ; but I can fairly say that our disagreements were on trivial matters, and openly confess that I, in most instances, was to blame for their occurrence. Like many more, I did not fully realise the value of my wife till I missed her from my side. "A good mother, an affectionate partner, a wise counsellor, a model of industry." Those words might have been written over her tomb in all truthfulness. She lies buried in Finchley Cemetary, near her son, and

Peace to her ashes.

She was the daughter of a small farmer of Harefield, and spent her youthful days in service, her maiden name having been Sarah Thrift.

On reaching London, we were poorly off, and had not the wherewithal to furnish a room. An acquaintance, whose marriage was postponed, however, lent us the furniture he had managed to get together. When his marriage took place, the furniture was given up, and we had to sleep on the boards. Still, she was equal to our misfortunes, and the way she improvised a suite of furniture can only be realised by one who has seen "Our Flat."

How she laboured at the press and assisted me in the work of my printing office, with a child in her arms, I have no space to tell, nor in fact have I space to allude to the many ways she contributed to my good fortune.

During my stay at Eton, my earnings averaged thirty shillings per week. As may readily be imagined, I had been enabled to save but little, the balance between receipts and expenditure going in improving my wardrobe and paying the loans I had contracted in the interval between the expiration of my apprenticeship and my successful tramp to Eton.

On my return, I did not waste much time in Uxbridge ; I saw that my chances of obtaining employment were nil. I determined to try London. Enquiries told me that I had fallen on evil times. The railway mania had suddenly collapsed. During its height, printers in London had been coining money. As a natural consequence thousands rushed to the new El Dorado, then the tide receded, and strewed upon its shores lay hundreds unnoticed and uncared for. I at once saw my only chance was to get into the country as soon as possible, where my all-round abilities, I imagined, would be sure to serve me; but before going, I thought I would join the society of compositors, I wasted two days in the attempt, and ended by getting robbed or losing my indentures, without which it was difficult to enter.

It was three o'clock on a summer's afternoon in 1850, when, disgusted with my chances of obtaining employment in London, I determined to try my fortune elsewhere. I decided to make for St. Alban's that night. My walking powers were nothing to boast about and I should have fared badly in a long distance race. Still, I managed to cover the journey ere the day was spent, and after resting for the night, I determined to visit the abbey and see what few remains existed of Old Verulam.

The task of showing me over the abbey devolved on a dark-eyed, rosy-cheeked, maiden, a year or two my junior. I was tolerably well acquainted with the abbey's history, and the leading questions I put to her soon attracted her attention. It is not vanity which prompts me to say that we had not proceeded far before I knew that she was more than usually attentive to her visitor. The signs of this were more apparent from her endeavours to hide them. How long we continued to saunter through the old abbey, I do not know; but that my stay was treble the length of that of ordinary visitors and possibly more, is beyond doubt. We had inspected everything worthy of notice, many of them twice over, and were about entering the second time on the origin of pancakes, which, legend tells us, were first manufactured in a portion of the abbey buildings, when, looking round, I saw the verger advancing. For my part, I would sooner have seen the devil. Not a word had been spoken, save on subjects connected with the abbey, and yet, why did she, and for a matter of that, myself also, get so flush about the cheeks as the disturber of our pleasure drew near us? Shaking off my confusion, I told him how pleased I was to have the opportunity of visiting a structure so full of interest, and of which I had read so much. I was not sorry on discovering that I had struck a chord in pure harmony with the verger's thoughts, the result being that my stay lengthened, and I was favoured with yet more accurate accounts of the history of the abbey. About saints I have my doubts, but that an angel once walked the aisles of this particular abbey, I am ready to make an affirmation any day in the week. After bidding the verger and his daughter good bye, I struck through the pathway that led to the site of the few remains of Old Verulam.

After I had satisfied myself with seeing everything of interest in St. Alban's, I directed my course to Olney, took a glance at the home of Cowper, and from thence to Bedford. While in this neighbourhood, I was interested in making my acquaintance with the cage in which the author of the "Pilgrim's Progress" was once lodged. From thence I passed on to Northampton, Kettering, Leicester, Market Harborough, occasionally journeying out of my way to inspect places of interest. My companion on the road from Leicester to Market Harborough was none other than a "sha'low cove," one of a class of persons who dispense with every vestige of under clothing in order to excite pity and alms. During the time we were journeying together, I was both amused and instructed by the strange stories he told of his adventures; and the tricks played by men of his class. But these I have no space to recount. I found on entering Harborough the walls posted with a proclamation forbidding all meetings in favour of Chartism. With my last penny I entered a beer shop in the Market Place, the sign of which, if I mistake not, was the "Pied Horse." While seated in its clean and sanded tap room, I could not help reviewing my position. Homeless, penniless, wanting to sell my labour; but finding no purchaser. To quote a couplet from one of my own poems,

"A desert bounds my view to-day,
    A sea of ice to-morrow."

Vainly I strove to restrain my tears, it was all to no purpose. They rose higher and higher, and eventually broke their bounds;

they gave me relief, though scalding my cheeks in their passage. In answer to their inquiries, I told them the exact position in which I was placed, that I was a Chartist and ready to brave the legal authorities. They admired my pluck, and I was tempted to keep my seat till the evening, when their numbers considerably increased. My capacity to amuse them, won their good will, and the way in which I disposed of an opponent to Chartist principles, made them my sworn friends, so much so, that they voluntarily paid my night's lodging ; thus helping me out of a difficulty that I had long pondered over. After closing hours, I found myself alone in company with my antagonist. He told me he was in no way opposed to Chartism, and asked if I would breakfast and dine at his expense on the morrow. This offer I was only too glad to accept, and in the afternoon we inspected the Catholic institution, then newly built. On our return to his place of lodgment ; he offered, if I would stay the night over, to pay my bed, breakfast me, and accompany me on the road to Derby. It was mid day ere we parted. On separating, he gave me all the halfpence in his possession. I entered Derby on the day of the opening of its Arboretum, from which I saw Green ascend in his grand Nassau balloon, which on two occasions I had helped to lower.

I stayed for the night in Derby, visiting its various printing offices in search of a job, but without success, and, hugging the shore of the river Derwent, made for Matlock on the following morn. I had read the whole of Wordsworth's Sonnets and, penniless as I was, I enjoyed the journey. After a night's rest in a common lodging-house, for which accommodation I paid twopence, I started for Uttoxeter. I found the roads heavy, and the privations I had suffered, rendered me so weak that I made little progress. While climbing a somewhat steep hill, my attention was attracted to an organ-grinder seated on a bank that bounded the roadway. I soon perceived that he was in the act of eating, and, on approaching, saw that he had alighted on a bed of wild strawberries. To his evident dissatisfaction, I seated myself by his side, and began to share in the feast. He did not utter a word, but by his appearance I plainly saw, that he looked upon me as an intruder. For this, I cared little. Assuredly, I thought, as a breakfastless Englishman I had as much right as an Italian to this feast of Nature's providing. "Never talk with your mouth full," says the old adage, and this command was strictly adhered to. I rose refreshed and pursued my journey, leaving him, like Oliver Twist, thirsting for more.

On entering Uttoxeter, I succeeded in gaining a few pence trom a fellow printer, and spent the same on a saveloy and a ha'porth of bread, which served me for a dinner. After visiting the Market Place, and inspecting the statue raised thereon in memory of a well-known incident in the life of Dr. Samuel Johnson, I thought it wise to secure a bed as I intended to stay in the town for the night. I knew it was a case of Hobson's choice, and in a short time I might have been seen seated in the common room of a padding ken, conversing with its proprietor, who had agreed to furnish me with a half bed for twopence. I had been to every printing office in the town, was tired and footsore, and had parted with my last penny. I had not been so seated long, when a traveller entered, and took a seat by my side. Instinctively he seemed to know the position in which I was circumstanced, and asking for a pot, commenced brewing from tea taken from a screw box. Then from a capricious pocket, he drew forth bread and butter. In the meal thus provided, I was asked to join. Need I say, that I was too hungry to refuse. In a conversation which ensued between my friend and the keeper of the house, I learned more than I cared to know.

"How have you been getting on since I last stayed here?" enquired my friend, "Oh! badly;" was the reply. "The fact of your having the fever in the house spread, and the place was deserted in consequence," but the unfortunate affair is partly forgotten, and customers are returning."

"Have you seen or heard anything of Poll or Bet recently?" inquired the traveller.

"Not just recently," was the reply.

"Bless them. They saved my life, and I shall never cease to remember their kindness. Had they been my sisters, instead of strangers, they could not have done more. Instead of seeking ground that would have paid them better, they were content to work the neighbourhood, and share their earnings with me. At the risk of their lives, they nursed me, did my washing, and, at their own cost, brought me dainties that alone could have tempted me to eat. Bless them! bless them! say I. I had a hard struggle; but, thank God! I am better, and shall be able to push along now."

The shades of evening closed in, and my companion signified his intention of retiring to bed.

"We'll sleep together, if you don't mind!" said he.

To this, I reluctantly agreed.

The bed allotted to us was on the stair landing. In it we slept soundly till daybreak, when my bedfellow told me he was bound for Rugeley Market, and asked me if I was going in that direction. It was decided that the way would suit me for Birmingham, and my friend immediately suggested that I should breakfast with him, and then start in company.

During the journey, he narrated his life adventures. In early youth, he had worked at a large factory in Birmingham, where he had been tempted by a lad a trifle older than himself to visit a neighbouring wake. On returning to work the next morning, he was astonished to find himself charged with stealing the till belonging to his employers, and for which he ultimately suffered ten years' transportation. Rightly or wrongly, he assured me that of this crime he was entirely innocent, and I believed him then and believe him now. He admitted that he had shared the money, but had taken no part in and was entirely ignorant of the robbery. After we had covered some three miles, one of my feet began to fail me, and, finding my company was only hindering him, I suggested that he should proceed alone, leaving me to get on as I best could. Soon after, I might have been seen, seated on a bank by the roadside, nursing my lame foot. While so seated, I remembered that it was my 23rd birthday. The outcome of the fairy palaces I had built during my apprenticeship was to find myself an outcast. Severed from home, with not so much as a penny in my pocket to enable me to communicate with mother, wife, or to enquire how my poor sick boy was faring. While so seated, a market cart belonging to the Duke of Newcastle chanced to pass. I hailed its driver, and asked for a lift, which he kindly gave me, and, with him, I rode till I reached Rugeley.

"I will get you to mind the horse while I get shaved," said he, as we entered the town.

On leaving the barber's shop, I saw he was bleeding like a stuck pig. This arose from a grog-blossomed face, the result of living too well, I imagine. Before parting to meet my friend at the Market Place as agreed, the driver treated me to a glass of ale and a crust of bread and cheese, for which I was extremely thankful, for I had had neither bite nor sup since morn. I soon found my friend, the ex-transport, who told me the market was a failure, and that he did not intend to hire a stall and exhibit his wares. We cordially shook hands, and I saw no more of the man who befriended me. I made my way to Tamworth, and thus got an inspection of the residence of Sir Robert Peel, the son of a successful neighbouring cotton spinner. From Tamworth I passed on to Walsall. The afternoon was nearly spent when I reached it, and I determined to see the churchyard, where the key was turned on me while wandering amid the graves. I was suddenly tapped on the shoulder by a clerically dressed gentleman, possibly the rertor. I told him I was desirous of seeing the grave of any celebrity who might be buried there. He told me there was no one of any great importance, but that a Professor Faraday, formerly a journeyman bookbinder, lived or had lived within a short distance, and without solicitation gave me sixpence, and my release. The reason assigned for his lateness was that the choir was practising. I lodged in a neighbouring house, and started for Birmingham early next morning, when I expected a letter containing an enclosure from my friend Warwick, which I was fortunate enough to find awaiting me at the Post Office. Thus replenished, I entered the first eating house I came across, and got a hot meat dinner, a thing I had not had for many successive weeks. In the evening, I found myself in front of a small hall, and on a bill posted at its doorway I read that Mr. Passmore Edwards, the now proprietor of the "Echo" was about to lecture on the subject of "Peace." On entering, I found few listeners, and had no difficulty in obtaining a front seat. I thought the lecture a passably good one, and, on the following day, passed through Droitwich, and so reached Worcester. From Worcester I proceeded to Tewkesbury, where I did not fail to see its abbey, its bloody meadow, the house in which the young Prince is said to have been murdered, and the confluence of the Avon with the Severn. I had heard so much of this town from my old friend, Kingsbury, whose birthplace it was, that it seemed as though I had spent my life in it. From Tewkesbury I made my way to Gloucester, where I obtained work. I had not been long so engaged when I received a letter from Mr. Twelvetrees of Dunstable, for whom I had worked a short time, asking me to return and take charge of his business till he was released from a law court where he was engaged in a case in which a former employer of his own was interested. As I liked Dunstable and did not like Gloucester I asked to be released from my engagement. This was reluctantly granted, and I immediately took rail to Cheltenham, when, after staying the night over, I started to walk the remaining portion of the journey. As I was strolling through the streets of this once fashionable watering place, I fell across a bill that told me that Woolridge and his company were staying in the town, whom it will be remembered, I had befriended in my native place. I soon found my way to the theatre door; but had not the heart to enter, my object being to seek an engagement. I have often wondered what might have been the result had my desire been gained. My whole course of life would have been changed. I have over and over again tried to reckon up my chances of success. I had a good tenor voice, could sing, and, as I have since proved, was capable of interpreting the words of an author. The proof of this statement may be found in my reputation as a reader at the various clubs of London, and my success in this direction at Nottingham. True, I invariably recited my own poems; but this did not result from any want of capability to recite others. I still entertain my belief that I should have been a successful actor.

I obtained a cheap bed, and, was about turning in for the night, when I was startled by a somewhat strange noise. I immediately commenced to search the room, to learn the cause thereof. In a dark corner, I alighted on one of the strangest sights it was ever my lot to behold. It consisted of the mere trunk of a human being. Concluding that it was lifeless, I was about to take my departure. Thinking that it was best to be sure, I cried out "Who are you, and what right have you to be here?" The reply was, "I am Bristol Tommy." On farther enquiring, he told me he got his living by begging. I was so far satisfied, and as he told me that it was his nightly place of rest, I was satisfied to let him remain. Before going to bed, however, I thought it advisable to peer under the bed, when, to my astonishment, I found, it was converted into a stable for a dozen or more horses, but they were wooden ones, yes, there were my old friends "Dobbin," "Black Bess," &c., evidently forming a portion of a roundabout. These, I found, were the property of the lodging-house keeper.

I enjoyed my limited stay in the town of Dunstable, and from my singing and a discussion with a temperance lecturer was much favoured. The person in question, professed to give his life history—I was not long before I detected that he was confused in his statements. In appearance, he was about forty; but on reckoning up the years of which he professed to give an account, he must have been if my figures were reliable, a hundred at least. On rising to ask a few questions, I artfully put each separate statement before the speaker, for the truth of which he vouched. I then asked his age, to which he replied truthfully, and then confronted him with the fact that he had made out he was a centenarian. His friends seeing that he had been fairly trapped, invited me to meet him in the vestry of the Wesleyan Chapel in which the meeting was held. I complied, when to my astonishment, I was threatened with personal chastisement. After a deal of wrangling, the meeting was adjourned till the following night, when it was arranged we should congregate at the Temperance Coffee House in West Street. The lecturer failed to keep his appointment; but just as the meeting place was about to close, he entered to throw up the sponge, and confess that he was in error. In a short time after we were the best of friends, and in the time that elapsed before the company was informed it was time to separate, I discovered that the man I had opposed was a fine pen and ink artist, and a most companiable person. My temporary engagement closed, and I at once made for home, covering the distance on the second day after quitting the town; getting thoroughly drenched by one of the most fearful downpours I ever remember. On my entering into Rickmansworth, I saw an old woman driving a donkey, the cart attached being full of water. Jokingly, I enquired if she had given over her general carrying business and dealt in water only? Her answer consisted of a volley of abuse, and the information that she considered me a saucy puppy, which was undoubtedly more or less true. Still, as we were both drenched, she might have been content with a laugh. My intention of reaching home that evening was given up, and lodging for the night sought and obtained at the next beer shop, which bore the sign of the "Royal Oak," and in which Charles was pictured in full regal garb, and so seated that his pursuers' failing to capture him could only be accounted for by their stone blindness. Rising early, and putting on my soddened clothes with difficulty, I made for Harefield, where, after breakfasting with my wife's sister, and drying my clothes, I renewed my journey. On reaching home, my pockets were in the same condition as when I quitted it, and the devil might have danced a hornpipe in either without injuring a limb. Still, I was sound and heartily welcomed by my friends. I had travelled over a thousand miles and, despite of hardships, was safe under the old roof-tree.

Before quitting Uxbridge, there is an incident in my life that I desire to record. This occurred at the time I was residing with my grandmother. I used to sleep with my half-uncle, Tom Baker. There was only a thin partition between the bedroom we occupied and the bedroom of the adjoining house. Nearly fifty years ago, a terrible tragedy took place in the Waterloo Road, Lambeth. This was the murder of Eliza Grimwood, a female of great beauty and easy virtue. Suspicion fell upon a well-known tobacconist who was found innocent of the crime, then upon others, and finally upon a young man, the son of a neighbouring builder, named Huddard, a near relation of the victim. Shortly after his acquittal, the building of New Windsor Street, Uxbridge, was commenced, and the recently-suspected murderer was selected to superintend the carrying out of the contract. It so chanced that he took lodgings with Mrs. Duffin, the wife of a tailor, and so became the occupier of the room adjoining that in which I and my uncle slept. I was speedily engaged to clean the new-comer's boots, &c., and thus enabled to add to my scanty income. He was a portly, good-looking, young man, with nothing sinister in his appearance. In a short time after he became our neighbour, we were startled by his nightly ravings and self-accusations. From these we concluded he was guilty of the murder with which he had been charged. He would call her by name, re-act the tragedy, implore her to come back to him, and end with a prayer imploring forgiveness. This occurred nightly.

Shortly after my return to Uxbridge I was informed that the parson, the Rev. Mr. Price, had refused to read the burial service over a child that had not been christened. I thought, and so did many more, that, as the parents and their friends, had expressed their desire that it should be done, the parson acted harshly in declining. I, therefore, determined to attend the funeral, and, finding that the grandfather of the child, an old friend of my father and a neighbour, had determined it should be done, if not by the parson, by some one else, I volunteered my services. I and the child's grandfather completed the ceremony, to the satisfaction of all present, and many who were not. Whether or no its soul was admitted to heaven in consequence, or whether it was subjected to eternal torments, I leave those versed in such matters to decide. All I know is that by the part I played I helped to comfort the child's mother in her great distress, and with that I am satisfied. I then thought, and still think, that of the parson and myself, I was the better Christian.

I was then pressed by my friends to hold a Benefit Concert at the Town Hall. My objections were met with the statement that a person my superior in the social scale, had recently done so. My resistance was feeble from the fact that I saw no immediate means of replenishing my thoroughly exhausted exchequer. Having decided, I wrote to my Eton shopmates who at once offered to provide the printing free of cost. On learning this, I walked over to Eton. I was heartily welcomed, and came back some thirty shillings richer than I started. It occurred in this wise. While at Eton I proposed to raise a tramp fund by a weekly subscription of twopence each. The amount to be given to each wayfarer was two shillings and sixpence. At the time of my calling, the balance in hand amounted to the above-named sum, and it struck my friend Herbert that, as there was no immediate call upon the said fund, to propose that the amount in hand should be handed over to me, which, meeting with the consent of all concerned, was at once done. This fact and my own experience, previously narrated, should go far to prove there is little lost from setting a good example. At the termination of the Concert, I found myself in possession of forty pounds, and this would have been more than doubled had I not, from a want of forethought, selected the 5th of November, and the counter attraction of Van Amburgh and his lions. Still, I was more than satisfied. It was a larger sum than was ever before realised in the town for a like purpose by similar means. With this, I determined to start printing, and, fearing the money might slip through my fingers and be wasted, I at once set off for London, purchased press and type, and forthwith commenced. Carpenters built me frames, and a signboard and a facia writer, did all that was required in his way free of cost. My first place of business was at a chairmaker's in Windsor Street. I soon found the wooden press I had purchased was useless. It was built upon the same lines as that used by Caxton, and, judging from its appearance, had done the state some service. This was a sad blow; but, by writing

I discovered that those from whom I had bought it, were willing to exchange it for one of iron, if I was prepared to pay a difference of five pounds, to give me a long credit for the same if I accepted their offer, and, in return, furnish me with a Stanhope, very little better for working purposes than the wooden one I had returned. Its great fault was a hollowness in the platten. On enquiry, I found it would require six pounds to rectify this defect. As I could not raise so large a sum, I determined to do the best with it. I soon found that by getting a quantity of river sand, and placing it between the platten and the carriage, I could, with the necessary amount of friction, wear the surface level. It was a long, laborious task, as may readily be imagined; but in twelve months it was accomplished. I may here mention that my friend Herbert expressed a wish to join me on the termination of his apprenticeship and, on my consenting, he immediately forwarded me the whole of his savings, a trifle short of twenty pounds. My earnings did not average at first more than fifteen shillings per week, but, this did not cause me to despair, inasmuch as my customers continued to increase, and among them I had hooked a small auctioneer. About this time, the "Uxbridge Pioneer" was started. Its editors consisted of Gerald Massey, Kimber, Hudson, Gurney, and a few others, elected by the members of the Young Men's Improvement Society, indeed it was the offspring of the "Manuscript Newspaper" of which I was the proposer and joint editor. The first number was hardly in existence before a split occurred among its conductors, owing to political differences, and Massey and myself proposed to start a paper in opposition; but then came the question of how the money could be raised. We called together a few friends who were political sympathisers, and so raised the large sum of fifteen shillings, each subscriber to this amount moreover guaranteed to contribute one shilling per month towards future issues. With fifteen shillings paid up capital, we produced the initial number of the "Spirit of Freedom, and Working Man's Vindicator." Neither I nor Massey had possibly ever attempted the writing of an article before. Still, there was the number chiefly composed of our productions, and stranger still, it was fairly successful. We had read the "Northern Star" and most of the Chartist publications then in existence and possibly formed the idea that the effectiveness of an article was dependent upon the amount of treason it contained.

The contents of No. 1 excited strangely antagonistic criticism. They were highly praised as the naturally indignant outpourings of the wronged, and condemned as the venom of snakes; they were the words of patriots and of men charged with treason; they were full of wisdom and insanity. After a late perusal, I thought, taken separately, each class of critics was wrong; but, conjoined, fairly near the mark. It contained little calculated to instruct, but plenty of declamation and much if not the whole of the fierce declamation was warranted. The chief contributors were Massey and myself. In the introductory chapter we proclaimed it to be our intention to "Call a man a man, and a spade a spade," whereon an ironmonger wrote upon a shovel, "This is a spade," and stuck it outside his door. A witty baker travestied title and sub-title into the "Spirit of Mischief, or Working Man's Window Breaker." On the Sunday following the publication of the initial number, the parson thought fit to interlard his sermon with condemnatory illusions to its authors, and warning his flock not to be led astray by the inculcators of treason. In order to attract attention, Massey proposed that my brother Frederick, then a mere youth, should be dressed in imitation Guarde Mobile clothing—the reason given for the selection being that the civil corps of Paris had joined the people. How the clothing was obtained, I do not remember, but on market day my brother was so dressed and to be seen vending to the farmers, town and country people, the first issue of this terribly-in-earnest, treasonable publication. A curious mistake attended its printing, for which I was solely responsible. A day before printing, I had occasion to shift the press, and this led to my making the stupid blunder of starting the imposition from the right hand instead of the left. The error was not discovered till the entire edition had been printed. Gladly would I have reprinted the thousand copies; but I had neither the fifteen shillings necessary to purchase the paper, nor the means of raising so much. After a while, I hit upon the idea of printing a coloured wrapper, converting the back into the forage, and stabbing! If I was wild over the mistake, I was pleased with my mode of getting out of the difficulty. This, I have reason to believe, was the first English book ever printed Hebrew fashion. During the time we were engaged in bringing out "The Spirit of Freedom," a meeting in favour of Free Trade was announced to be held in the Town Hall. The purport of this meeting becoming known, Massey and my old friend, Farrell, determined to oppose, not in favour of Protection from a landowner's point of view, but from the Chartist standpoint on that question. The result was that both were refused a hearing, and the Free Traders successfully proved that they could be as unfair to opponents as Chartists admittedly were, and, to speak truly, all are, when it serves them. Our small journalistic venture continued for twelve months, and the only loss was the fifteen shillings subscribed, and my labour, or a part, that was never paid for. After eight or ten numbers had been produced, Massey, who had formed an acquaintance with Walter Cooper and Thomas Shorter, both lecturers, the latter of whom ultimately became the secretary to the Working Man's College, left Uxbridge to take a berth as secretary to the Tailors' Association, in Castle Street, Oxford Street. Within a month, I was at his recommendation sent for to take charge of a Working Printers' Association that it had been determined to start on the same premises, under the auspices of the "Promoters," a body of gentlemen who were known as Christian Socialists, who had been impressed with the Socialistic doctrines of the New Testament, and the unequal distribution of the wealth of this and other nations. The most noted of these were Professor Maurice, Lord Goderich, Vansittart Neale, the Rev. Charles Kingsley, J. F. Furnivall, and Thomas Hughes, the author of "Tom Brown's Schooldays." I accordingly came up to London and met Massey. In the interval, I had become aware of the fact that a Co-operative Printers' Association had been already formed by Archibald Campbell, in Pemberton

Row. On that rock I split. I mentioned the fact to my friend, and said I thought it inadvisable to start in opposition to those whom we ought to look upon as friends. He pooh-poohed the idea; but I was determined. At last, it was arranged that I should seek an interview with those concerned. I started on the mission, found they were struggling, and that determined me to join them. My plant was of great service, and it was then and there it was agreed that it should be joined to that with which the "Citizen of the World" had been printed, and which formed their entire stock in trade. I confess that doubts of my ability to manage a London printing office partly determined my resolution. At any rate, I had determined to be one of the rank and file, rather than a commander, as I undoubtedly might have been, and the result was that I had to be content to take fourteen shilling per week instead of three pounds as I might have had.

During the three years' connection with the Working Printers' Association I was taught many things, the first of which was not to believe that because a man preaches right and justice, he is bound to practice either. We were engaged in the printing of a work for Robert Owen. The pages of this as set were ordered to be stereotyped. The process was not so speedily performed in those days as now, and the result was that a considerable portion of the used font was eternally blocked, and the getting out of the work unavoidably prolonged. With this fact Alexander Campbell, senior, became necessarily acquainted. He was at that time engaged at an office in Aldermanbury, belonging to the promoters of a Canadian Railway. "You want capital, and capital you must have. I can negotiate a loan for you with the parties by whom I am employed." His offer was accepted and the loan received, would have been honourably met from the sum due from Mr. Owen. The bill for the sixty pounds was duly made out by Campbell, and accepted on behalf of the Association by our manager. By this time, our existence had become known to the heads of the Christian Socialist leaders, and by them we were given considerable support. The result was, hearing of our necessitous condition, so far as capital went, Mr. Thomas Hughes volunteered a loan of sixty pounds through Campbell. On informing us of the offer, he expressed his belief that we should be able to dispense with the other loan, the bill for which had been already signed; but for which we had never received a farthing, to which we agreed, and at his suggestion it was arranged that he, Campbell, should make waste paper of the document. To our surprise at the end of the term, that bill was presented. The hoary-headed old sinner who had patted us on the head and called us his children, had trapped us out of sixty pounds. He had had the money, and had spent it. This was not all, we soon found that the type in our possession had not been paid for, that the rent due amounted to some thirty pounds, and that all the printing plant was liable to be seized at any moment by the landlord. The demand was, I believe, met by Mr. Hughes, whom I have every reason to suppose imagined at the time that we were all concerned in the villiany. I was in a terrible rage when I first became acquainted with the treacherous act of the man who had betrayed us, and on his son, a working partner, attempting a defence of his father, entirely lost my temper, and threatened to use personal violence if he proceeded to urge any further excuse. We were, from causes already explained, much behind with Owen's work, and one day he called to express his dissatisfaction. We did all that was possible to appease his anger, but all to no purpose. On his expressing his determination to take his work to another printer, I reminded him of his own doctrine of man being the creature of circumstances and his opposition to rewards and punishments. The good old man, I imagine, saw the inconsistency of the part he was playing, smiled and departed. A considerable sum was due, and application was made for the amount. This again brought Mr. Owen to the printing office. He expressed his surprise at the contents of the letter, and declared he did not owe a farthing, inasmuch as his friend who had charge of the work, had paid for the work done. Despite of our assertion that we had never received a farthing on account of the work done, he expresesd his entire confidence in his friend's honesty. The money was eventually paid, but we never heard how his friend explained the deception he had practised on Mr. Owen or on whom the loss fell. I confess that these two instances shook my faith very considerably in the prominent men of the day, and I sat about to find a remedy, with what result I shall presently have occasion to show. From the paltry sum of fourteen shillings our wages or rather wages and profit now ranged from thirty shillings to two pounds per week, and this, in despite of adopting the nine hours' system. This was done at my suggestion, upon the ground that work ought to be fairly distributed, when work was slack, as it then was in the printing business. There was yet another reason urged me for its adoption, namely, the increased power of production, which should certainly tend to the lightening of men's labours. Men in regular work, should not work overtime. If there is more than they can do, they should give the chance to others. If this was done, the fully employed would be the gainers in the long run. Despite of an increased volume of business, the Co-operative Working Printers ultimately came to grief. The causes are of easy explanation. The associates could get no balance sheets from their manager. I had had enough of confidence, and determined to be in a position to judge of what concerned me or leave. Finding, after six months, in spite of my repeated appeals, I could get no statement of accounts, I, with John Dodd, determined to seek an interview with Mr. Vansittant Neale, who had taken the responsibility off the shoulders of Mr. Hughes. Mr. Neale listened to our complaint, expressed sympathy, but told us that in consequence of the then state of the law, there was no limited liability in those days, he could not assist us. He admitted we were fully justified in the course we had taken, and urged us to go on as before. This, rightly or wrongly, I was determined not to do. I then reminded him that I had supplied a portion of the plant, and, upon suggesting that I should be paid out, he at once aquiesced, I also reminded him that myself and friend had contributed weekly towards paying off the sum borrowed, and that as we left through no fault of our own, we were entitled to the sum paid, inasmuch as the party at fault would get the business and goodwill. He admitted the justice of this. But from the opposition of the manager, these just demands were never met. I confess that I was greatly chagrined at the result of my attempt to prove the practical value of the co-operative system applied to creative industry. What would have been a success was converted into failure by drink and, as was afterwards proved, positive dishonesty. We left and, as we prophesied, within five years Mr. Neale lost every farthing of the money he had ventured in the business. This was only one of many ventures of the same kind he had assisted, and in all cases the result was the same, the chief cause being found in the fact that the managers of most of them led a life of extravagance, drank deeply, and were subject to no official control. In many cases the associations were as trading concerns pre-eminently successful, or rather were known to possess all the elements or success had they been judiciously employed. In a few years after their starting the whole of these societies passed out of existence. It is worth while to pause and consider why they failed. There were doubtless many contributing causes, but the most important were internal. Neither managers nor associates were equal to the requirements of the new system. The elected managers, unused to power, started to live extravagantly. They sought each others' company, and at a tavern, and thus gave encouragement to drinking habits, till there was scarcely a sober man left among them. As for the associates, the majority cared for the success of their associations just so far as they served their interests. In order to prove that I am not libelling them, I will mention a single fact that fully substantiates my statement. After getting co-operative prices for their labour they refused to purchase of each other. The shoemakers went elsewhere for their hats, the hatters went somewhere else for their shoes, and so on, because they thought they could get them cheaper. This was fully established at a council meeting. For the credit of the printers, be it said, that this lamentable statement in no way applies to them. They were only four in number all told; but the statement furnished proved that they had spent more with the tailors and shoemakers than associations numbering hundreds.

During the three years spent in co-operative working, I had led a life of considerable activity. In political matters, as a Chartist, I was seldom idle. If I was not on the platform, I was engaged in council or scribbling an article or a song with a political purpose. Both Massey and myself on arriving in London were able to command a leading position. Nor were my efforts confined to political matters only—I became a regular contributor to the "Christian Socialist," a weekly journal, edited by J. M. Ludlow, and afterwards by the Rev. Charles Kingsley. I attended meetings whenever desired to propagate socialistic views.

The reading of "Alton Locke" had led me to the belief that its author had genuine sympathy with the working class in their struggle for political independence. Hence it was, that on entering the printing office one day, I felt compelled to tender him my gratitude. Whether I committed a blunder in my mode of doing this, I know not; but, I know that his reply was the reverse of what I had expected. I know that I was urged on by my feelings, and that whatever I said was prompted by respect and genuine admiration. His reply was to the effect that I had misunderstood his motives in writing the work in question, and, in a word, that he did not require my thanks. I confess at the time I felt hurt, and puzzled. The hurt soon healed, and the feeling to which the rebuff gave rise passed away; but the puzzling nature of the reply remains till now a mystery. I have found my satisfaction since in reading the whole of his wonderful works, and shown my gratitude by a very wearisome pilgrimage of a score of miles on a terribly hot day to his shrine and dearly loved home at Eversley. Had this great author told me he never intended to disturb the game laws by writing and publishing the verses in "Yeast," under the title of "A Rough Rhyme on a Rough Matter," I could not have been more astonished than when he told me that I had judged wrongly his intention to serve Chartism in depicting the

Tailor Poet. Could he have realised how closely the hero of his story resembled myself, how nearly he described me when he pictured Alton Locke, as a cross between Burns and a mongrel, how closely my hopes and aspirations resembled those of the fictitious character he had drawn, I feel assured he would not have spoken as he did. It was out of the fullness of my heart that I spoke, and I believe that I had no right to be considered impertinent. I would all praise to authors was equally honest.

During the time I was with the Co-operative Printers, we, like other firms, had our periods of slackness. In order that we should employ these dull periods profitably, I proposed we undertook to reprint "Uncle Tom's Cabin." The novel was then being run through the weekly issue of an American journal, under the title of "Life among the Lowly." This journal by chance fell into my hands, and struck by its transparent merits, and remembering there was no copyright law to prevent us, I had faith in the speculation. On a council of the associates being called to decide on the matter, I failed to carry my proposition, and had the mortification to find that those who had afterwards hit upon the same idea, realised an almost fabulous profit.

The chief object of the leaders of the Christian Socialist Movement was to organise supply and demand, and thereby prevent waste.

With nothing but memory, no "dairy," as the Tichbourne witness swore, to guide me, I find I have missed a material part of my story. In the interval that occurred between my return to Uxbridge and the concert, I paid a visit to my aunt Bean in London, with whom my sister, Betsy, was then living. When about to return home, it struck me it would be well to undertake another search for work. On the morning following, I crossed London Bridge on my way to the Southern coast. Hugging the Thames, I passed Greenwich, Woolwich, Erith, Gravesend, and so reached Dartford, where I obtained employment. This I soon found to be very unprofitable. The font ran short of sorts, and I was so often brought to a stand-still, that my earnings barely sufficed to keep me. This resulted in a demand for better pay, which, not getting, I signified my intention to leave. The apprentice vainly urged me to stop, even going so far as to offer to pay the difference, telling me he was a ward in Chancery, with more money than he could spend. I heartily thanked him for his offer, but respectfully declined to avail myself of it. While making my way to Gravesend, my attention was attracted by a skittle-alley outside a roadside publichouse. This I entered, and was busily setting up and knocking the pins down, when two strangers entered. They had barely seated themselves, when the elder of the two challenged me to play for a pint, a challenge which I at once accepted. " Sixpence I beat you," said my opponent eagerly. I replied I would wager half that amount, and, with that understanding, we commenced to play. The same bet was repeated on the successive games, when, eventually, my opponent confessed himself broke, the total of his loss amounting to, as near as I remember, fifteen shillings. While resting on the settle, his companion drew my attention to his mate who was crying. " He is fairly ruined," and then he proceeded to inform me that he was a basket maker, and the money staked and lost was his sole working capital.

" Then he ought not to have risked losing it," said I.

However, after turning the matter over in my mind, I could not bear to think that I should be in any way the cause of his downfall, and so returned the money, saving the price of a crust of bread and cheese. Bidding the loser and his friend good day, I continued my journey, and, reaching Gad's Hill, where I had seated myself on the embankment, I hailed a traveller, who, wanting a rest, sat himself down beside me. In the conversation that followed, I found he held Socialistic and Chartist views. He then proposed we should share a pint of porter. To this end, we clubbed pennies. Whether Dickens dwelt hard by at the period, I do not remember. Our conversation led to a desire not to part company, and the result was a toss up as to who should turn back. This I lost. He told me he had been engaged by a music hall proprietor in Chatham, which suggested to me that we might earn a joint living as singers, to which he assented. No sooner was this agreed to, than he evidently became desirous of testing my abilities in this direction. I suggested that he should begin, and in a baritone voice he started to sing "The Bell-ringer." Seeing that I was not inclined to praise his singing, he said that reciting was his forte. "Then, give me a taste of your qualities in that direction," said I, when, fitting an old pair of spectacles and pulling a front lock over his forehead, he commenced reciting a well-known speech from "The Hypocrite," ending with "I'll dish them all, for I'll wear a spencer." This was at least a creditable effort. I thereupon was called upon to fulfil my promise, which I did by singing Lover's well-known song, "Come to the West." We reached Gravesend in the evening and found the place full, it being the day on which Westall performed the task of walking twenty-one miles within the seven hours. This great feat was performed on the turf. At night we set to work at our new business; but it resulted in an utter failure. Meeting one engaged in a like manner, he at once expressed a desire to join us, saying that he was a favourite pupil of the well-known teacher of elocution, Vandenhoff. Regardless of this important recommendation, we signified our dissent to the proposal. In the morning, while at breakfast, we mutually came to the conclusion that we could do better separate, and, thereupon, determined to part company, his final act of friendship being a proposal to mend my breeches, which he performed.

When climbing the hill that leads to Canterbury, I enquired of an old lady, named Greigg, if she could inform me where the encounter took place between the followers of Mad Tom and her majesty's troops sent to capture them, when she pointed to the wood lying to the left, and informed me that she lost two sons in the affray. As we were passing a roadside inn, she told me it was within its walls that the inquest on the leader's body was held, and, entering, I was offered a lock of his hair, or, at least, hair of some sort, which I declined to purchase, believing it to be a simple trick to raise money. In passing Rochester, I had spent my last sixpence, in viewing its cathedral, and vainly strove to get the relief given nightly to six poor travellers. Thus it was that without a farthing in my pocket I entered the city of Canterbury. I got relief from the trade, slept at the "Golden Boot," and early next morning took my way to Margate, with two other travellers. Hearing that an old farm house was partly composed of the ruins of a ruined abbey, I and one of my companions determined to see its interior if possible. On telling its owner that I was visiting all such places in order to describe them, we were invited in, treated to biscuits and a glass of wine. In the midst of our feast, his son arrived, and from his treatment we soon discovered that our presence was not wanted. To shorten my story, I may simply note that we in turn visited Ramsgate, Margate, Broadstairs, Deal, Dover and the intervening towns till we reached Ramsey where we parted company. They going on to Brighton, of which they were natives, and I striking inward to Maidstone. When I reached London, I was both footsore and hungry. I, therefore, made for my aunt's, where I was kindly treated, and for home, which I reached on the following day.

It often occurs that when one of the toiling class exhibits superior speaking or argumentative powers to his fellows, he is chosen to be their advocate. Practice makes perfect, and, in consequence his services are more required. Possibly, the time and trouble thus occasioned are not to be borne without payment. In a life's experience, I never knew a pleader of this kind get rich, while, on the other hand, I could name hundreds who died paupers. If called to take part in settling labour disputes, his very name stinks in the nostrils of the employing class, and they shut their workshop doors against him as they would their own doors against the plague. By the general public and I am sorry to say in these are included many of the class he has been struggling to benefit, he is looked upon as a dangerous demagogue and vile self-seeker, and by the advocates of the rich and newspaper editors in their service, as a dishonest knave, whom they would readily consign to prison. These latter shut their eyes to the fact that there is little difference between their own position and that of those they condemn.

The only differences are that the latter are better paid for their services and have richer clients, for what are newspaper editors but paid advocates? I have, moreover, heard members of the legal profession condemn the poor man's advocate, as though it was more honourable to take fees from an oft-convicted villain than to be paid by honest working men who only demand justice. The council who took his oath that Courviorsier was innocent, after he had confessed himself guilty, was thought good enough to be made the recorder of one of our chief cities. The workman's advocate is very generally branded as a moral leper. Fortunately, as a rule, he is not a coward.

With the exception of two separate occasions in which I was engaged to do liberal election work, and for which I admit I was well paid, two pounds would cover the whole of my earnings as a labour advocate, and this trifling sum I should never have received had it not been for George Hunter Mantle declaring to the Council of the Reform League that he would speak no more without payment, not because he wanted to be paid personally; but because he held it an act of injustice to call on favourite speakers for their services without compensation for their loss of time and useful advocacy. The funds of the Reform League were never extensive; but, in recognition of the justice of his views, the council passed a resolution by which two shillings was awarded for each speech delivered within a radius of four miles of the chief office, and eight shillings per day and railway fare to those sent to more distant parts. When legal advocates and hypocritical leader writers are prepared to work for such prices and make like sacrifices, they will be in a better position to fulminate their inconsistent libels.

When I entered London, in the early part of 1851, Chartism was in a parlous state. Its old leaders were discredited, or rather divided, and their forces dispirited. On Fergus's death, Harney and Jones fought desperately for the position he had occupied. Harney and Fleming, the last of whom dealt in social rather than political matters, got possession of the "Northern Star," while Jones, in rivalry, started a paper of his own, successively named "The People" and "The People's Paper." The struggle did not last long. The "Northern Star" was no longer a name to conjure with. Finlen turned henchman to Jones, on promise of a weekly wage, he never got. Jones made me a like offer; but that I respectfully declined. My business required all my attention; beside, had I not shown my dislike to paid advocacy and paid advocates, and had I not started the "Propagandists," a combination of intelligent youths, pledged to speak whenever required free of pay, and did not my friend Mr. George Jacob Holyoake, slate me for this in his "Reasoner?" I do not attempt to justify my line of action. I know it was honest and was forced upon me by deeds done by former advocates that I should do no good by naming. They died long since and let their evil deeds sleep with them. With this small band of self-sacrificing young men, I assisted to keep the old flag flying till, at length, they formed the nucleus from which sprang the Reform League, to the Council of which I was almost unanimously elected a member. It was chiefly officered by men whom I had kept together, by those who took leading parts in the discussions held weekly at the "Windsor Castle," Holborn, from whence came Odgers, Cremer, Howell, Applegarth, Davis, Henriette, and others of lesser note. The story I have told is the only warranty for saying that the leaders lived upon the people and were instigated by selfishness. To me it seems doubtful if the apostles themselves could have worked for a lesser payment. Of the movement under the generalship of Edmund Beales I shall have to speak elsewhere. That it was the outgrowth of the Chartist movement, there can be no manner of doubt, that it was more successful is likewise true. Its action begat the necessary rivalry to cause the parliamentary leaders of all parties to bid for popular support, and the result was the adoption of a franchise that closely assimilates that which formed the foundation stone of Chartism. When Disraeli robbed the Whigs of their clothing, he was forced to the act by the submergence which threatened him and the party he led had he receded. The credit or discredit of any act belongs to him or those who force another or others to do it, and especially when the act itself is opposed to his or their will.

This is as true as that the gardener may justly claim to be the grower of the tree the seed of which was sown by him, and moreover prepared the soil in which it took root and flourished.

When Haynau arrived from Austria he appears to have been better known than he imagined. His flogging of women had become known to the lowest and least informed of our countrymen. One of his first visits was to the brewery on bankside belonging to Messrs. Barkley and Perkins, and from its employees, a class of men who pay little attention to politics, he met with a reception, equal to his merits. The men of beer chased him off the premises, and he took refuge in a dust-bin belonging to a neighbouring inn, from whence he escaped after receiving a sound flogging. The English people were delighted with the brewers, and in order that they should be able to express their feelings on the matter, a meeting was called at Farringdon Hall, at which my friend, Mr. George Julian Harney was the chief speaker. Never shall I forget when, in the midst of his speech, some hundreds of the workers in the brewery invaded the hall, every man armed with a whip that he carried over his shoulders. Long and continuous shouts greeted their arrival.

The last man hanged for attempted murder was one, Walsh, a travelling tinker. This took place at Chester on August 27, 1861. Regarding this incident, it is not generally known that a reprieve was granted, and that by some unexplained mishap it miscarried. It so happened that a Mr. Skidmore, with whom I, as a printer, had business relations, undertook to clear out the office of a solicitor in Westminster. Among its contents was the document in question. To this he directed my attention, and ultimately offered to sell it for a trifle, which offer I accepted. If my memory does not fail me, Lord Grey was Home Minister at the time, and to the same document his name was attached. The genuineness of his signature I was in a position to recognise, while the remaining signatures and seals were sufficient to test its genuineness. It would be curious to know why this reprieve never reached its destination. I parted with this precious document to an old friend, whom I was given to understand, was offered a large sum for the same, an offer that he did not accept. On his death, I offered to repurchase it for ten times the sum I had sold it for, but though it was diligently sought for, it was never found by the members of his family.

Walsh was hanged in consequence, while, had the reprieve reached the chief official of the gaol, it is certain that he would have been spared.

When Fergus O'Connor died, it was thought desirable to hold a public funeral over his remains, and, to this end, it was necessary for the committee appointed, to get possession of his body. I with William Jones, once known by members of the Chartist body, as the "eloquent boy," and a cousin of the deceased leader, whose son fired at the Queen, had to wait on Dr. Tooke, at his establishment at Chiswick, and in whose keeping Fergus was at the time of his death. We soon learned that the Dr. had looked on the Chartist leader as a friend rather than a patient. We knew also that he had received little by way of payment for the great care and attention he had bestowed upon him. He readily consented with our wishes, told us many amusing stories of the deceased, regaled us, and, on leaving, presented us with half a sovereign wherewith to drink his health.

It cannot be truthfully said that I had joined the London Chartist when I saw a meeting announced to be held on the old tilting ground, Clerkenwell Green. The meeting was addressed by Sharp, Williams and O'Daly, the rostrum was a lamp post. I was about to follow when an army of police constables and detectives swept the Green. The people were terrified and fled. I was new to such sights, and I foolishly concluded that the people were cowards. Shortly after, I was standing on the pavement discussing the Irish question, when, a disguised policeman gave the order to move on. I said I saw no harm in thus speaking, and the reply was a shove, I still kept my ground, when he commenced to belabour me with a truncheon, that he drew from his flannel jacket. This I stood till the blood fairly poured down my face. It was fortunate for him, or me, that I had no weapon of defence. A fire breaking out in a Whitechapel sugar refinery helped to clear the Green. For the part they took in this meeting, Sharp and Williams were convicted, both, if I remember rightly, died while in confinement from the severity of their treatment. I followed them to their grave, O'Daly had the good fortune to escape. I made my way to the fire and spent the night at a small coffee house hard by, where a lot of low boys were engaged playing push penny. I had no money to pay for a sleeping apartment.

In 1854 or 5 a movement was started by the members of the Progressive Carpenters, of whom George Potter was the chief, in favour of reducing the hours of toil to nine. In order to favour their views they determined to offer a prize. I resolved to compete, although I was not aware of the particulars thereof until twenty-four hours of the time for reception of copy expired. By working hard I succeeded in producing a rough copy ere daylight closed, and during the night, I managed to change it into a presentable form. This was short work, considering it had to fill sixteen 8vo pages of brevier. Each contribution had to be signed with a nom-de-plume, and the name of the writer enclosed in a sealed envelope. The contest resulted in a tie between my contribution and another, and the chairman was called upon to give the casting vote which he did in favour of an essay written by his brother! Being made acquainted with these particulars, I determined to forestall them, and setting my people to work, I succeeded in placing my essay on the market within a few hours, the result being that ere the essay to which the prize was awarded had been distributed, the demand was satisfied. My sale reached close upon ten thousand copies, realising the sum of sixty pounds. My action in this matter was universally commended, more especially by the members of the society itself. I was afterwards informed by a member of the committee appointed to decide on the merits of the contributions, that by the influence of the chairman, he had been induced to vote for the essay to which the prize was unfairly awarded. It had been looked upon that the profit arising from the sale of the winning essay would more than repay the prize and all incidental expenses. Instead of this, the affair proved a serious loss. That, so far as I know, was the origin of the short time movement as it affects adult labour. The main line of argument was that with so much labour-saving machinery at our command, there was no necessity for more than nine hours' labour per day from any single person, and that is unanswerable. Whether or not a yet lesser term of labour would suffice, I leave others to decide. All I ask is that this reduction shall be first fairly tried. If working men were free agents, I would ask for no enforcement by legal enactment, but knowing they are not and never can be, with unrestricted competition and a crowded labour market, I would give to the workers the protection which legality alone affords. The fact that they have already been provided with the ballot to protect their right to vote will ever furnish a strong argument in its favour.

Among others with whom I became acquainted through my connection with the Christian Socialists was Mr. J. F. Furnival. I remember in the winter of 1852 or 3 being called on to address a meeting of wood-cutters at a public house room. On my arrival, I found that my colleague, Mr. Furnival, the now well-known scholar and critic, had arrived. The kindler-makers were on strike, and had made an appeal to the promoters of Working Men's Associations for funds to start a co-operative company as fire wood manufacturers. After the chairman's speech had ended, one of the strikers was invited to say a few words. His speaking powers proved to be far greater than we had anticipated. He was a man of a low type of countenance, and if there be anything in the belief that we all, more or less, resemble an animal of some kind, then he was undoubtedly of the fox order. A resolution in favour of the wants of the men being passed, I was asked by Mr. Furnival if I would accompany him on the journey home. The snow lay thick upon the ground, the storm had not yet ended. As we walked along arm in arm, our conversation turned upon the night's work and experience. The first question asked of me was regarding the speaker alluded to. I expressed openly my suspicion of his honesty. Mr. Furnival was otherwise impressed, and declared that he had determined to find the assistance necessary for the venture. "I am poor, Leno, miserably poor," he said. "True, I am a barrister; but without a brief. My income is solely due to the kindness of my father. If I fail in all other attempts to raise the necessary funds, my friend, Edward Vansittart Neale, will lend me the sum on my library," which he gave me to understand was worth one or two thousand pounds. "If you do," I replied, "mark me, you will lose it. A man with such an expression of countenance is not to be trusted." Whether my advice was taken or not, I never heard, but, if so, then I feel certain my prophecy was correct, as I must have learned something of the society's history. At that period, Mr. Furnival was a vegetarian, and informed me that his food was principally figs. The weak and fragile form by which he was characterised did not induce me to follow his example. In truth, I concluded he would be all the better for a few chops and steaks. Still, weak and short lived as he then promised to be, I am pleased to learn that he is yet living, and that on vegetables or beef he has done good work in his own special department of literature. That he was earnest to do good, I can readily testify. When the Working Printers' Association split asunder, I lost touch with Mr. Furnival and his friends, with the exception of Mr. Thomas Hughes, with whom I could never claim but a slight acquaintance.

My expressed opinion of the Deptford orator who had won the confidence of Mr. Furnival, may have been from the merest prejudice; and totally unwarrantable; but I have found impressions so created are generally correct, though by no means infallible, and hence, to place too much faith in them, is to be, at least guilty of injustice.

My knowledge of Herzen "the great-souled Herzen" as the "Spectator" once dubbed him, was not great. We met once, twice or thrice at the International Meetings (the first international) that were held in a cafe, kept by a French exile in Chapel Street, Oxford Street. I can only picture him as a firm set man of stoutish build with an English expression of features. He evidently had a better knowledge of me than I had of him.

"You are a printer, Leno, are you not?" he said to me one night as we were leaving Jacques', in Chapel Street.

"Yes," was the reply.

"And have type and presses of your own?"

I nodded assent.

"Then, he continued, I think we can work together." He informed me that he was then engaged in flooding Russia with revolutionary literature in the form of leaflets, and asked if I would mind running an underground printing office?

I said I would do so willingly, and we parted with the understanding that we were to meet again in order to make the ne necessary arrangements. I never saw him any more. I then knew he was an exile; but I did not know that he had been a state prisoner in Siberia, or if I did, I have forgotten it. Every man who had fought or suffered for freedom, no matter where, was a hero in my eyes, and I can safely say that I was ever ready to assist all such to the extent of my power and ability.

The International to which I allude was, I have been informed, started by my friend, George Julian Harney. I became a member of it in 1848 or 9. Harney was more conversant with foreign politics than any man I ever knew, and the first inquiries made by foreign refugees on landing on our shores was to forward the discovery of his whereabouts.

My knowledge of Carl Marx was limited. I met him on several occasions nevertheless. I remember in the year 1855 at a public meeting called at the instigation of the Reform League. At its conclusion, Marx, Odger, Cremer and several others adjourned to the parlour of a tavern in Chancery Lane where we held a kind of committee meeting. His daughter, since a well-known writer, was with him on the evening. Like Herzen he was, physically a stout and apparently robust man. He was deeply interested and a firm believer in the social doctrines, he never ceased to advocate, and for which he so often risked his liberty and life. George Eccarius, a fellow countryman, who materially assisted him in his literary labours, was for many years friendly, and I followed his remains to their last resting place. He was a man of remarkable intellectual attainment and power, and like myself, edited for a time, the "Commonwealth" newspaper. He contributed one or more articles on Natural History to the "Times," for which he got payment. In an after conversation with me, he referred principally to the nightingale, he proclaimed it to be a habitat of Africa, and asserted that in its passage to this country, it passed over the shallowest portion of the channel, or rather over the last porsion of land submerged, as its ancestors did before ever it was separated from the main land. At the time of which I am speaking, he possesssed a caged nightingale that sang during the daylight, which he offered to me as a gift; but I preferred to reject the offer, as I felt sure it would soon die if under my charge. He was an excellent linquist, and when he told me that he had received his education, at the cost of the ecclesiastical fund sequestrated by the small state to which he belonged, I could not help contrasting the wisdom of his ancestors compared with that of my own.

In nearly all the political and social movements of the working class, I have taken my share of duties. I may not have played the leading roles; but they have never been of the humblest kind. With the Christian Socialists I was a representative, on many occasions, as the delegate of the body of which I was a member. In the Chartist movement, I was almost in all cases elected as a delegate; in their meetings I was seldom left out as a speaker. I was an active member for the committee appointed to meet Kossuth, Garibaldi, and in the movement to honour Shakspeare. I strove hard for the abolition of of the liability of the goods of poor tenants for rent, for limited liability with regard to investments, for the spread of education, and for the abolition of drunkenness, though I was never an abstainer. Rushed to the assistance of Joseph Arch and his friends to aid the agricultural toiler, and my voice was to be often heard pleading their wants in the Home Counties, whereever opportunity served. If my tongue was silent, my pen did not forget to make known my sympathy. I was intimate and friendly with almost all the working class leaders of the day and, the best proof I can give of their estimate of my sincerity and ability, is the fact that at a great meeting at the Memorial Hall, Farringdon Street. I stood in the foremost rank of those selected as future fitting working class members of the House of Commons, whenever they had a desire to elect one or more candidates. True, I was never called on, but the reason for that might easily be explained, despite of the fact that many more successful men had to be content with a much lesser number of votes.

I am reminded that I once wrote some verses on Swearing, the copy of which I forwarded to J. M. Ludlow, then editor of the "Christian Socialist." They were duly inserted, with approval? Certainly not. As they were published, I have no copy. Despite of the fact that, after-reflection convinced me that it was unwise to put them in the way of publication. I still feel that they do not contain a single word of untruth, and that the truth they contain should be recognised by the well wishers of humanity. However repulsive the ordinary language of Drury Lane may be, it is the language its inhabitants have been taught, and they speak it as naturally as a Kaffir speaks that of his people. I have fairly shivered when listening to them, nay, more, I have been stricken with horror. Aim to make it more refined by all means. Let us hope this is being done by the influence of our School Board. I have watched the actions accompanying the words used in this district and those of others, who employ less adjectives, and I do not see that they materially differ. Indeed, it has often struck me that those of the latter proved the more dangerous, and the more detestable. "Strong words break no bones" and "soft words butter no parsnips."

It may be that I have been like the man immersed in a bog-hole who comforted himself with a smelling bottle." Here I saw and see one side of society as it exists, and a pitiable sight it presents. Are these foul-mouthed men and those still more foul-mouthed women to teach and educate the mothers of the future? Are those staggering wretches, reeling reprobates, called mothers, those brutalized fiendishly selfish swines of men to be allowed to reproduce their like under the same hellish conditions for ever and ever more? I have noticed that royal visitors are never allowed to trespass in these regions, so perhaps it is as well that I and others who have been trained to think have been forced residents. It, at any rate, prevents their existence being forgotten. I could never have written the "Crowded Court," or "A Modern Inferno" had I not seen with mine own eyes, again and again, all that I have endeavoured to picture in these two poems. As these may not be within the reach of every reader, I will take the liberty of merely directing their attention to them.

The graveyard alluded to is now a playground for street arabs, and I am proud to say partly through my exertions. This is how it occurred. One day, I received a letter from Mr. Hasting Hughes, brother to Thomas Hughes, then M.P., and the author of "Tom Brown's School Days," asking me if I knew of a plot of waste-ground in a crowded neighbourhood, that could be purchased for a playground for poor children, as he had a lady friend, Miss Octavia Hill, who was desirous of employing a certain sum in that direction. My thoughts reverted to the disused graveyard, and the result was its purchase. The necessary preliminary inquiries were my sole contribution. By a curious coincidence, I saw the last interment in this "God's acre." I was on a visit to the metropolis, and while passing down the Lane, I heard the report of musketry. It was over the grave of a soldier. That I have since been informed was the last burial.

Born and reared in the country, it has been my lot to reside in and about Drury Lane for a considerable portion of my life. Use is second nature, and in despite of the fact that there is no spot in London where a more low and degraded class exists, I had no special desire to shift my quarters. I confess that I had no inclination to enter into any close relation with them. I was neighbourly, and that was all. They were a mixed lot of persons; but by no means all bad. Indeed the larger portion consisted, and yet consist of honest, industrious working men and women. There were and are thieves in abundance; theatres being their happy hunting ground. This is no more than might be expected. Despite of our costly police arrangements, the thieves seemed to do pretty well as they pleased. It so appeared to me from the fact that I have known professional thieves living in the district, carrying on their knavish trade for over half a century without being detected or charged. I am informed that when a covey of birds are disturbed, the practical sportsman invariably covers a selected bird, and, if a first-class shot, is almost certain to capture him, dead or alive. So these evil birds of this fallen district should be singled out. They can be easily identified by the fact that they never follow an honest calling. A writer in the "Athenæum" once expressed wonder that I was able to write true poetry in Drury Lane. Why not? If I am able to write it at all? Any artist will tell you that there can be no good picture without a shadow; and that, in no few, it forms a chief factor. The green fields, the woodside where I gathered blue-bells and violets, the sparkling Colne, in a word, the haunts of my childhood, do not lose from my seeing them from my garret, and the music of the birds that haunted them seem sweeter from the horrid oaths by which my ears are so constantly assailed.

I am pretty generally accredited by shoemakers with being the first to start a trade journal devoted to their interest, but this is a mistake.

All that I can lay claim to is that I was the first to make such a paper a success. The credit of priority belongs to James Dacres Devlin and John O'Neill. Unfortunately for them, the initial attempt failed. Still the credit of initiating a shoemaker's journal is not mine, and I would be the last to rob them of it. They were both men of remarkable talent, and both well acquainted with the art of boot and shoemaking. Indeed, it is generally conceded that as a workman in his own special department, that is as a closer, Devlin has never been excelled. This belief is strongly supported by the closing of the "Shamrock Tongue" which, till lately, remained in my possession. Both Devlin and O'Neill were Irish, and their literary capacities can be judged by the numerous works they have left behind them. The autobiography of the latter I take to be an interesting and truthful picture of a workman's life in the first half of the 19th century. At the end of nearly twenty years as proprietor and editor of "St. Crispin," I was reduced to the necessity of selling my interest therein for the ridiculously small sum of sixty pounds. In a commercial sense, my fault was the invariable support I gave to the men. I did this with my eyes open, and continued it after I saw that it militated against the success of the journal, more especially in the advertising department. Still, with the workers and not with profit-mongers lay my sympathy, and I trust ever will, and I could do no other. It was not business; but it was natural, for was I not of their order? and did not Christ, ye Christians, pursue a like course? I shall merely repeat the old proverb, "There are none so blind as those who will not see."

While proprietor and engaged in conducting "The Westminster News," I was wont to employ a County Court reporter, named Beaver. He was a real Bohemian in his way. He had been schoolfellow with Charles Dickens. There is one statement of his that I can vouch for, namely, that Dickens never forgot his old friend. On more than one occasion, I had letters in my hand which had contained small accounts from the great author, which their holder would ask me to cash. Whatever else he might have been, this Fred Beaver was an original. In his life he appeared to have run the gauntlet of all the hells of London, and to have mingled with most of the notorious rakes who haunted them in his younger days. He appeared to have been well-known at Belchers', Spring's, and the rest of the sporting houses, Mother H.'s, the Finish, and a welcome companion to the Waterfords and others of that ilk. On more than one occasion, I have heard him claim to be the original Dick Swiveller, and, whether he was or not, to that strange character he bore a strange resemblance. Full to repletion of snatches of old songs, strange toasts, and witty sayings, jaunty in his manners, shabby in appearance, but very genteel, he was withal an amusing mortal. If he sat for Swiveller's portrait my readers will be pleased to learn a little more about him. As may reasonably be expected, he lost caste, and eventually turned blackmailer rather than reporter. For this he was prosecuted by Madame Rachael, and sentenced to a long term of imprisonment. He in due time escaped, his prosecutor taking his place for extracting money from a foolish old lady whom she had succeeded in making believe that she could "make beautiful for ever." The imprisonment told on Beaver's constitution, and the sporting " kens " rang no more with his hunting and less reputable songs, although he is known to have lived for a few years after. He was a creature of the time in which he lived, and his prototype would be as difficult to find now living as the majority of those immortalised in the pages that fill the various volumes of his old friend and schoolfellow.

During the early fifties, when Lord Palmerston was premier, it became known that a body of French workmen was about to visit London, and a committee was formed to provide for their reception. The committee was composed of Messrs. Wall, Finlen, Murray and others. Unfortunately they were void of funds. Still, they had to be raised somehow, and steps were taken to this end. Morley, Palmerston and others likely to assist, were, in turn, visited. The interview with Palmerston was a remarkable one. On seeking admission to the premier, the purpose of the visit having been stated, the members of the deputation were invited in.

"Well," said the noble lord, "who and what are you?"

"I am Tommy Wall, the Chartist," said that member of the deputation.

"Well, Tommy Wall, the Chartist, what is your errand," at the same time digging Wall playfully in the chest.

Tommy was equal to the occasion, and said that their visit was to obtain money, accompanying the words with like friendly digs.

These were mutually indulged in through the entire conversation that followed, the end being that Palmerston signified his approval of the idea, and contributed a good round sum. Tommy was familiarly known as Cannibal Wall, from the fact that he lived on his mother, or rather at his mother's expense.

During the existence of the Reform League, I was called upon to speak at a public meeting announced to be held in the Saint Pancras Vestry Hall. On climbing the platform, I found myself seated by Washington Wilks, who was to propose a resolution which I was to second. On Wilks rising, he commenced to speak with his usual eloquence. Suddenly, I observed him stagger, and stretched forth my hands to save him from falling. I was, however, too late. He was picked up and taken to the small Vestry Hall when it was found that life had expired. " Punch " once facetiously remarked it could dispose of Wilks with a pin. This sudden death proved that not so much as a pin was necessary. This tragic event terminated the meeting, and it was reported that on visiting his home, its cupboard was found bare of a crust, and, on searching his pockets nothing was found but a fusee ! So ended poor Washington, the author of the " Life of Irvine," and the compiler of the History of the " Half Century," and the sub-editor of the " Nonconformist."

In a political sense, I have always belonged to the advanced guard. In my early days I plead guilty of advocating physical force. This I did, from a belief that the use of such force was justifiable ; but I only advocated it when there was a fair chance of success, and I have invariably opposed it since the working class won possession of political power. I have yet to learn that I acted wrongly. I am fully satisfied that events have justified my belief in the principles of " the People's Charter." True, as a movement it died out ; but it died to live again. The points unwon are sure sooner or later to be legalised, saving Annual Parliaments. That members of Parliament will be paid, I feel assured. When I belonged to the Liberal Caucus, none but lawyers were prepared to contest the Strand district in the liberal interest, and if anything in politics be certain, it is that few of this class will be found to venture the expenditure of a thousand pounds without they see its return and at least a fair margin of profit. I do not advocate a great wage, certainly not more than two hundred pounds a year, nor would I compel persons to take the same who preferred to give their services.

With regard to Socialism, I feel persuaded there is justice at the bottom of it. There is, however, no well thought out or rather, satisfactory scheme, and its advocates seem to me too eager. It is coming peacemeal, and Lord Wemyss is correct in saying that traces of it are to be found in all or nearly all our more recent legislation.

James, or "Jimmy Acland," as he was usually called, a few months previous to the election of 1868, carefully marked the changes Disraeli's bill were likely to affect in the English constituences. The results were placed before the heads of the liberal party, and it was at once determined to test their accuracy. For this purpose, it was ultimately decided that the leading men of the League should be employed. On hearing of this, and that we were to go in pairs, Odgers at once decided to pair off with myself, and that we should select his native county, Devon. The committee objected to this arrangement, saying two good men could not be together. In common parlance it was to be a good man and a duffer. The result was that I was conjoined with William Worley, a man quite as experienced and clever as myself. The arrangement was that we should report the whole truth and nothing but the truth, and if we found a constituency likely to return a working man, the liberal party would bear the expense and assist his return. With this understanding we started for Guildford in Surrey at once. On pursuing our enquiries, we discovered that Guildford Onslow had but a poor chance. His opponent had been nursing the borough, as it is termed. Meeting Onslow, on Castle Hill one day, I went boldly up to him and asked what views he held regarding his chance? He eyed me with suspicion and returned an evasive answer. I then produced a letter from Mr. Gladstone telling him my mission, when he gave a more satisfactory reply. We ultimately visited Chichester, Winchester, Southampton, Christchurch, the Isle of Wight, and other constituences, sending reports from each, thirty-three in all. What we learned was clearly stated, and the advice given followed, the result being what we prognosticated, with one or two exceptions. In the end we got a letter from the liberal whip, that none had guaged events with equal accuracy, and he should treasure our returns. I could fill the whole of the space at my command with our adventures, but I have only space to say that at the time of the general election, I was chosen to be the parliamentary agent of Mr. George Howell in the Aylesbury division, for which he had been advised to stand. This resulted in his losing by a majority of a little over two hundred votes, which alone was due to the want of the ballot. We were short of money, and had no means to bring our supporters to the poll, and, in this plight, had to meet Messrs. Smith and Rothschild, both bankers and millionaires, and the unnatural coalision that had been arranged between the liberal and conservative candidates.

I had read Lewes's " History of Philosophy," his " Goethe," a series of articles in the " Cornhill," if I remember rightly, on Pond Life, as seen by the aid of a microscope, and his contributions to " The Leader " newspaper. I had moreover seen the play written in conjunction with the late Charles Matthews. and I had formed the conclusion that he had few, if any equals. My friend, Stevens, had also informed me that his annual earnings by contributions to high class periodicals was not less than £1000 a year. Passing down Wellington Street, in company with my friend, we ran full butt against this noted man, and I was introduced to him by my friend. After a hearty shake of the hand, we adjourned to the Bell, 'where with his friend Pollard, the bill poster, the late Emperor of the French, used to fleece the unwary. Lewes was a person so far as I remember, below the medium height, and anything but an Adonis; his face being deeply pitted by the small pox. He was a big radical and expressed his sympathy with the political and social work I was engaged in. In a few weeks after, on paying a visit to my friend, Thornton Hunt, I met Mrs. Lewis at his apartment at the corner of Maiden Lane. She was seated on a couch, reading proofs of leading articles, that had been written for the " Globe " if I am not mistaken. She was a short, stout, luscious looking personage, and had, so I was informed, separated from her husband on a yearly allowance of two hundred and fifty pounds. This was, of course prior to his close relations to George Eliot. Whatever views may be formed of this connection, there can be no doubt that the public reaped profit thereby. To Stevens I owe a like introduction to Dr. Kelly, to whom I once made a proposal for the establishment of a Literary Art Union to encourage the production of useful works ill-calculated to pay expenses, with which proposal he heartily agreed.

Just after the breaking down of the Hyde Park railings, I received a circular from a well-known member of the Reform League calling upon me to attend a meeting at the " White Horse," Rathbone Place, in order to meet M. Cluserat. On my arriving, I was shown into a private room, where I found a dozen or more of my confreres. The chairman announced the purport of our being called together. It was none other than to create civil war. Cluserat who followed, said he was in a position to command at least two thousand sworn members of the Fenian body, and, on our consenting to join him, would act as leader. I was the first person to attempt a reply, in which I denounced the proposal, stating that, if proceeded with, it would surely lead to our discomfiture and transportation. I, moreover, stated it was my firm belief that the government would surely be made acquainted with our secret. In the next day's "Times" I was not astonished to find a detailed account of all our doings, not entirely accurate, it is true, but sufficiently so to show that the reporter must have been present. The speech I made was put into the mouth of George Odgers, his own speech being favourable to the views of the French adventurer. I noticed while we were discussing the matter that only a match board petition divided the room we occupied from a room adjoining, from which the sound of voices could be plainly heard, and declared my intention of getting out of the place as soon as possible. Others agreed with my view of the matter, and the room was soon cleared of those present. The name of the traitor was never satisfactorily known, butI think it was none other than Robert Hartwell? who was at that time the real editor of the " Bee Hive " newspaper, for which George

Potter, assumed the credit. Finding that his scheme had failed, Cluserat made his way to Paris, and instituted the war of the Commune. I was fully satisfied with the success the Reform League had met with, and, being opposed to civil war on grounds stated elsewhere, I was bitterly opposed to the interference of Cluseret and his Irish followers.

By chance I knew Robert Owen's secretary, and used to be in the habit of visiting him at his employer's offices at the room rented of William Stevens, in Wellington Street, Strand. One room was filled with letters the socialist leader had received. Many of these were from our present Queen's father, the Duke of Kent, but I remember being shown one that I felt far more interested in. This was a letter from Godwin, the author of "Caleb Williams." It was almost solely respecting his adopted daughter, by Mary Woolstencraft having been run away with by a young poet, named Shelley. Evidently the writer was in a lachrymose state, and as it stated, so too was the mother. This struck me as being exceedingly strange when I remembered the particulars of the connection between Godwin and the celebrated Mary Woolstencraft. The young lady in question, it will be remembered, became Shelley's second wife, and was the author of "Frankenstein." It was the duty of Rigby, Mr. Owen's secretary, to hunt up the Prince of Wales, in order that he might get part of the debt due from the Duke of Kent. One day, by appointment or otherwise, he sought an interview with the Prince at the Admiralty Office. While seated in the vestibule he noticed the mast and cords connected with the telephone. Feeling curious to know how this was worked, he rose from his seat and commenced to pull the lines. In a second, a naval officer rushed into the place and soon let my friend know he had done wrong. With many oaths, jumping about like a parched pea, he told him that he had signalled to the officers of the South Coast that they were to prepare for sea, as the French were about to attack them. All the while he was busily counteracting the order. My friend, Rigby, described him as a short man, with a grog-blossomed face, and as being in a terrible rage. So friendly was the Duke of Kent with Robert Owen and so enraptured with his social doctrines, or professed to be that he made overtures for placing his daughter, our present Queen, under his charge, and, among others, I was shown a letter from him to this effect. There is, however, great probability that this was written solely with the view of getting further advances from Mr. Owen.

I have often expressed my surprise at the stupid ideas that have taken deep root among men who claim to be sensible. For instance a man makes a speech in the House of Commons, and he obtains credit for being a clever orator, but a speaker of greater ability at the Cogers or other place set aside for debating purposes, is called a spouter or as one having the gift of the gab. The motives of the former are seldom questioned; those of the latter are set down as condemnable. It has been my lot to hear some of the finest speeches both in and out of parliament, and I confess that I have never heard finer than those delivered at the " Blue Post," in Shoe Lane, and the "Green Dragon," in Fleet Street. Where did the present Attorney General first air his oratory but at the "Belvedere" discussing Forum? where Dan O'Connell, Bronterre O'Brien, George Thompson, but in discussions of a like character? Surely the surroundings are neither the speech, nor its inspiration. The truth is that I have heard speeches in Parliament that would have disgraced either of the halls I have mentioned. In the latter, I have listened pleasurably and profitably to Richard Hart, James Hanney, the author of "Singleton Fontleroy," John Clarke and many other equally clever men, who had neither the money nor the influence to carry them into parliament. The only distinction I can draw between the two classes of speakers is that the majority of those of the House speak as mere nominees in support of speculators in bonds, railway shares, water shares, brewers, distillers, army, and navy interests, and the others for love of speaking, and a desire to forward their own particular notions. The mere fact that one speaker may have got three shillings a night to lead the debate does not militate against this, as a fairly truthful statement. I have, I confess, spent many happy hours and taken a prominent part in such debates. For this, I may be ridiculed; but it must be in company with Daniel O'Connell, Thomas Moore and others of like calibre.

Were I inclined, I could say much in favour of old fashioned taverns. On the other hand I should feel a difficulty in finding a good word for their successors. I do not blame the tavern keepers for this change; I know full well the alterations that have taken place, and the impossibility of carrying on business on the old lines. Johnson and Washington Irvine, both of whom had a large experience of tavern life, spoke well of them, and I see no reason why they should have done otherwise. Were either or both of them yet living, I feel assurred their words of praise would be changed to those of bitterness. Tavern parlours have ceased to be a source of profit, nor are they ever likely to again become so. Their old frequenters have died off, never to be replaced.

Although too young to remember the intellectnal gatherings and merry meetings that are well-known to have been of frequent occurrence at the "Turk's Head," and other once noted taverns, I can readily picture them, for although it was never my lot to mingle with men of equal talent and power of entertainment, I have done so with those who possessed no mean ability, and who, moreover, had been trained in the same school, and had found out a way of making their leisure moments pleasant. In my tavern life, I was no butterfly. The "Falcon" at Uxbridge, the "Castle" in Holborn and the "Harp" in Russell Street, satisfied me, and in their parlours, I spent my evenings for nigh forty years. The assembly, that met was somewhat of a mixed character; but most of them were of good conversational powers, thorough men of the world, and all more or less skilled as musicians, singers, actors, or writers. Sometimes the conversation would be of a political nature, at other times on the drama, and at other times of a bantering nature. The days when leading actors spent the spare times in taverns had passed away; still there was a goodly assemblage of men belonging to the second and third classes. Indeed the "Harp" company was of a peculiar character, and it would have been imposible to have found its match elsewhere. Broken down showmen, wild beast collectors, bankrupt country managers, coaches for the universities, scene painters, comic artists, chorus masters, dictionary compilers, theatrical property makers, playrights, private detectives, broken down orators, wild animal tamers, circus masters, and nondescripts of all kinds—liberal-hearted men who, when in clover, thought of little else but getting rid of the money they had collected. In this room and the others I reigned as a king and was accounted as a good all-rounder whether in a chaffing match, social entertainer, or a political debater. Whenever the house changed landlords, I went with the usual fixtures, though I am afraid the money I spent did not contribute largely to the making of either's fortune. Whips round were of frequent occurrence, and I have seen as much as twenty pounds speedily collected to set a hard-up frequenter of the "Harp" on his legs again, so that charity is or rather was not confined to the goody'goody race. Granting the truth of the old proverb, the sins of these tavern frequenters, these wild Bohemians, were not a selfish race.

Among others I well remember Ward of the giant memory, who appeared to have remembered everything he had read; Rennie who carried in his pocket an entire classical library, and who, after confronting all the scholars would usually wind up in a Bow Street police cell; the Scotch Dominie, Johnson, whom we christened "Ante-penultinate," the pedantic seller of worm powders, known as the "Isosseles Triangle," Yankee Palmer, one of the first to Jump Jim Crow, Davis, who could retail the entire series of lectures delivered at the geological and the rest of the museums, the father of the Vokes's, one of the joliest of mortals; old Weston, who had played with the elder Keen, Phil Benjamin whose sister ruined the great actor; O'Brien, the ex-consul, and orator; Ross who received £180 from the proprietors of the "Quarterly," for a slashing article on Gladstone's "Homer;" Pettit, Paul Merritt and others.

Till I had reached an age verging on fifty, I made little or no effort for turning my capacity to write into a means to attain a living. Then, in consequence of my son's illness, death, and the falling off of the bookselling into which I had ventured, I saw no other alternative. True, I had long conducted the "St. Crispin," a journal devoted to the leather trades, but then it was my own property. At the time of which I am speaking, I had sold it, and entered into an agreement to edit and conduct the same for its purchaser, for the weekly payment of two guineas. For a short period I undertook to sub-edit a social journal belonging to and conducted by the Rev. H. Solly. This, so long as it lasted, added a trifle to my income. Strange as it may seem, the chief of the paid literary work done by me has been relating to technical matters, of that to which I was most inclined and best fitted, I made no effort to find and never by chance attained, or very rarely.

Most of the unfortunate proprietors of papers started in the interest of liberalism, readily accepted by aid ; but had not the wherewithal to reward me for my services. I had had too much experience of the losses of such ventures to feel either surprised or discomforted.

My literary life, if such it can be called, has been a strange one. The first publisher of my works cheated me. I distinctly told him I would undertake to send copies to the press for notices. On settling up, a serious deduction was demanded on that head. I repudiated the charge, but to no purpose. All I could do was to write "settled and done" to the account.

I then became my own publisher, but the continual shifts I had to make caused that to fail. The wholesale houses would not follow me. Still, I continued to print, and I continued to sell through the reviews I got, enough to enable me to rub on with, aided as I was by my contributions to the press, though I confess the whole thus earned did not amount to a large sum. My work on practical boot and shoemaking brought me sixty pounds from the publisher. I received one hundred and more as electioneering agent for Mr. Rickman, when he stood for the Uxbridge division of Middlesex, a yet larger amount for my exertions in aid of the liberal cause in 1868. As a careful man these sums helped me considerably.

On a Sunday afternoon, when invited to tea by Thornton

Hunt, I was prompted to ask him whether he preferred Shelley or Byron as a man, and which of the two was the more liberal ? As I expected, he decided in favour of the former, and by way of illustration related an incident that occurred while in Italy.

"On one occasion I had to fetch or take to Byron some copy for the paper which my father, himself and Shelley, jointly conducted. I found him seated on a lounge feasting himself from a drum of figs. He asked me if I would like a fig. Now, in that, Leno, consists the difference, Shelley would have handed me the drum and allowed me to help myself."

Among others, I possessed the acquaintance of Stothard's son. As an artist he failed to wear the mantle of his gifted parent. I found him to be somewhat eccentric in his habits, and, if report spoke truly, of cantankerous spirit, but confess this, so far as I am concerned, rests upon hearsay. He was fully impressed with the idea that a man's character was betrayed by his nose, and in order to prove the worth of "Noseology," he issued a series of drawings of noses. At the end of his career he was an inmate of the Charter House, but from it he was discarded in consequence of his striking a fellow pensioner. Of this quarrel I know little or nothing, saving from the account given of it in the newspapers which stated that both the combatants were old enough to know better, both being octogenarians. He was wont to blame his father for his ill fortune or want of artistic success ; but in this I think he must have been mistaken.

I first met him at the "Constitution" with his friend Thirlwall, where it was my happy lot to spend many pleasant evenings. Among others who used to assemble there was Carl Rosa, then in very low water, Muddy Water Smith, a bass of some position, Mr. Waterhouse, the naturalist of the British Museum, Charles Sloman, the improvisitore, Thomas Miller, the author of many novels, and many other choice spirits.

"The Conspiracy to Murder Bill," brought forward by Lord Palmerston in 1858, after Orsini's attempt on the French Emperor's life, caused considerable emotion in England. The passage of its first reading in the House of Commons by two hundred majority, put the English people on their metal, and active steps were at once taken to oppose its further progress. In that opposition I took part. It resulted in the overthrow not only of the Bill; but the ministry. I knew Dr. Bernard, who was tried in England for the crime for which Orsini suffered, and many a time took part in the debates that used to be held at Wild's Coffee House, Leicester Square. I knew likewise Mr. Thomas Alsopp, who was also suspected to have taken part in the conspiracy by furnishing the conspirators with funds, and well remember his coming to my hotel at Aylesbury in his anxiety to learn the prospects of Mr. George Howell when contesting that borough. The last time I had the pleasure of meeting him was shortly before his death, when he took an opportunity that offered, of calling on me at my bookshop in Booksellers' Row, where we parted after a glass of wine at Carr's. This friend of the great Coleridge was a tall, well-built man of intelligent features and gentlemanly bearing. Bernard was defended by Sir Edward James, and it was undoubtedly mainly to his eloquent address to the jury that Bernard owed his acquittal. Unfortunately for the reputation of this great pleader, he fell into disgrace and had to quit England. On his return, I remember meeting him at Mr. James Acland's, Buckingham Street, on whom he had called to consult concerning his candidature for Marylebone. Acland knew full well he had little or no chance, but as he phrased it, he did not care to desert an old friend. The result was as this wily political agent predicted, James was beaten, and little more was ever heard of him either politically or otherwise.

Acland, I discovered, was a fellow townsman of my own, his father having been the host of "The Crown and Treaty hotel," the house in which the treaty was held between the Royalists, and Cromwellians. His life was somewhat strange and adventurous. He, on quitting home, took to the stage, and in his capacity as a player, took humble parts in conjunction with the great Edmund Kean. Afterwards he started at Bristol a radical paper entitled "The Bristolian," the publication of which is said to have led up to the riots. The afterwards celebrated orator, Henry Vincent, was in Acland's service at this period.

On Vincent's giving notice to leave, his old employer inquired what he intended to do. Turn lecturer, was the reply. Acland laughed at the boy's presumption; but it proved to be none, for Vincent became possibly the greatest lecturer that England has yet produced. George Dawson and Ernest Jones, were remarkable lecturers, but I must award the palm to Vincent, the compositor. His pictures of the Pretender and his battles were so marvellously and vividly drawn that under the spell of the lecturer you could hear the sound of the great man's jack boots. In after life, when a very old man, Acland restarted "The Bristolian," but, as might have been imagined, it proved a failure. To that, I acted as a contributor. The decease of the journal was quickly followed by that of its originator.

When Lord Palmerston died, I issued a pamphlet on his life which sold ten thousand copies, at one penny each. This was written from an antagonist's point of view, and realised a fair amount of profit.

When the League was at the height of its popularity, it caused a meeting to be announced to be held in Hyde Park. This the authorities thought fit to declare illegal. We thought otherwise and determined it should be held. The procession to start from the chief office, Adelphi Terrace. As we were proceeding at its head along Regent Street, our president, Edmund Beales, his friend, Colonel Dickson, and a few others of its aristocratic supporters, expressed a desire to turn into Gunter's, and the result was that the cab in which myself, brother, and others were seated, headed the procession. The police were drawn up in front of the Marble Arch, and of these we demanded admittance, which was denied. We then signified our intention of breaking through. This we tried, to be laughed at. While arguing the question with them, my friend Humphreys noticed the rails would stand no pressure, and, forthwith commenced to sway them backwards and forwards, assisted by crowds of persons in attendance. The result was as might have been expected, they fell. The police tried to resist the inpouring of the crowd. Simultaneously the people forced a passage from Knightsbridge and Park Lane, the former being led by Mr. Charles Bradlaugh.

The meeting then proceeded as it had been announced, under the Reformer's Tree. When it terminated, the police acting wisely, the crowd dispersed without bloodshed. The next evening saw another meeting called. Before its commencement, however, it was thought advisable that a deputation should wait upon the Home Secretary (Walpole), inasmuch as it had been whispered that the government were determined to oppose it. I was one of the deputation appointed to attend from the Council of the League. On its being pointed out that if the police or military shewed themselves bloodshed would ensue. With tears in his eyes, the ministers' accepted our offer to clear the park, and he on his part asserted his willingness to see that police and soldiers should be hidden from sight. On this understanding we left, and Odgers and myself hurried off to fulfill our promise. From the seats which served as a platform we announced that the meeting would be held in Trafalgar Square, of which meeting I was chairman. This was of short duration and all ended quietly ; or nearly so. Then followed the appeal from Cluserat, particulars of which I have previously detailed.

On Garibaldi's arrival in England, a deputation was appointed to wait on him of which I was a member. Waller, a well-known painter, asked myself and Odgers to use our influence to get him an introduction. The time was six in the morning, and we told our friend to meet at the rendezvous and take his chance, as there was a great likelihood that one or more would not be present. Our surmise proved to be correct. To his expressed desire to take his portrait, Garibaldi replied that he could give him no formal sitting; but if he liked to come with others while he was taking coffee he could do so. It will be remembered that for state reasons the liberator of Italy was hurried away. On hearing of this, Waller suggested the loan of the cape or coat, in order that he might complete the portrait. Garibaldi promised to return it. This promise was kept ; but it never reached the painter. Garibaldi remembered your humble servant and the series of lectures we were engaged to deliver at the hall on Saffron Hill. I have still a letter from him from Caprera which I greatly prize. This recalls to my mind a friend, young Bontem, who left England and, while in his service, after having braved many perils, was accidentally shot, alas! poor Yorrick! I knew him well.

In 1873, or about, coal rose to almost a fabulous price, and many of the extremely poor had to go fireless. I had recently been speaking in Lincolnshire and Cambridgeshire, where my attention had been directed to peat as a fuel. It suddenly struck me that it might judiciously be adopted as a substitute for coal. I forthwith placed myself in communication with an inhabitant of the district, and arranged with him for a continuous supply. At the onset, it was an unmistakable success, and ere a fortnight had passed, I had opened no less than seven shops in different parts of London. At first I got good peat, the lasting quality of which was almost equal to coal. It was, moreover, forwarded as ordered; but I soon found the quality deteriorate, and to add to my discomfiture, the Great Northern Railway seemed to take a delight in irregularity. I was moreover astonished to find that I was charged demurrage that took away all my profit, inasmuch as I could not get it carted from the rails. So with the inferiority of the peat supplied and the base tricks played upon me by the Company, I has fairly beaten out of the market.

John Frost and his confreres, Williams and Jones, obtained a remittance of their sentence, but Frost alone determined to avail himself of his freedom to quit the Australian continent. He arrived in England in September, 1856, and started lecturing on the horrors of convict life. We organized a right royal welcome for him on his reaching London, in which I played a prominent part. In recognition of my activity in the matter, he sent me his portrait shortly before his death, per Mr. George Odgers, who had occasion to visit the ex-transport, at that epoch of his eventful life. The Newport riot, of which Frost was a leader, was not wise; but the intention was at least patriotic, and for that reason, his self-sacrifice will ever remain green in my memory.

While a member of the first International, and seated in the upstairs room at Jacques' Coffee Shop, our proceedings were disturbed by the entrance of Felix Piat, and an Italian confrere.

They had been travelling all night to escape arrest, and we were asked to retire in order that they might go to bed. I could not help noticing the Italian patriot, for such was Felix Piat's companion. He stood full six feet high, and his face was scored with sword cuts. The next morning he started for Genoa on his patriotic mission, where he landed to find he had been betrayed. The brave patriot fought an army of gend'armes, and disabled sixteen, when he was surrounded and struck down from behind. A full account of his death will be found in Jones's paper.

For a spree, I and four others announced ourselves as candidates for the City of London, with no intention of going to the poll. We announced a meeting in Old Smithfield Market. This proved a failure, but we were told that Wakley and Sergeant Parry were addressing the electors on Clerkenwell Green, and in a short time we had stolen their listeners whom we entertained for fully four hours.

I knew many of the French refugees of 1848, and many a night I have walked the streets with them, I lived to see many of these unfortunate men return to their native land, and the recipient of high honours. A few never lived to return, of whom Monsieur Queval was one.

When Napoleon visited England in 1858, I was determined he should receive an appropriate welcome. I called together as many of the old and known Chartists as I possibly could. We adjourned after meeting at a coffee house then forming part of Middle Row, Holborn, long demolished. There I was asked to draw up a bill for distribution. This done, I was ordered to print ten thousand of the same. That bill I see has been copied in most French biographies. It was not intended to lead to any danger to Napoleon, but on reading it over recently, I could easily see how a clever councillor could make it neither more nor less than an incitement to assassination, especially if of the order of the solicitor who conducted the breach of promise charge against Mr. Pickwick. I shared the danger of their distribution in Cheapside; but did not get captured as my companions did. We knew full well we should be in a minority, and, for this reason, concentrated our force on two given points, Cheapside in the morning, and Long Acre on his return from the City, in the evening. The French refugees of London were not slow to obey the command to meet at the last spot. I have every reason to believe that they conspired for revenge for their expatriation, but for some reason or other it failed. The opinion held by the Chartists of this period, was shared by Lord John Russell, Gladstone, John Bright, and others of great though minor importance.

This, as might be expected was the chief theme of discussion at the debating halls of London, to which I was a frequent attendant, and speaker. I well remember making a speech in favour of regicide under certain conditions—those conditions included the subordination of a nation's troops for personal and unconstitutional ends, which I concluded by quoting Walter Savage Landor's spirited reply to the arch conspirator.

> We encourage assassins! Sir! Have no fear,
> No hold has the murderer or sympathies here:
> England loathes an assassin, and loathes him no less
> Whether shameful by failure or great by success —
> Whether hiding from sight, or set on a throne,
> Whether killer of thousands, or killer of one —
> Whether bribe or revenge, or the hope of a name,
> Or the dream of a "Destiny" "damn him to fame."
> Whatever the prompting, whatever the end,
> Has he slaughtered a people he swore to defend:
> Has he banded with ruffians, like him to strike,
> At a brother assassin—we loathe him alike!
>
> E'en where, Cain-like, by Providence guarded from ill,
> With a mark set upon him that no man can kill;
> Where prosperity seems all his projects to crown,
> We've no faith in his Favour—no fear of his Frown:
> Undismayed by his Fortunes unawed by his Fate,
> We smile at his "Destiny" Watch him and Wait.

At its conclusion, Richards, editor of the "Daily Advertiser" proposed that I should be thrown out of the room. To this I assented upon the ground that the proposer did it, no easy task and the proposer declined the invitation. That speech was undoubtedly quoted to the Emperor. Allusion in it were made to his oath breaking, his butcheries on the day of the Coup-de-etat, his bastardy, his immoral life, his forgeries. It was well known that there were French spies in the room, and hence the speech was made hotter than it probably would have been. William Carpenter, editor of the "Sunday Times," was the Grand, if I mistake not. Tallendier, now in the French parliament, Felix Pyat, who recently died after a stormy political life, and at whose grave I intended to have been, but broke down in my attempt to walk thereto ; Tchorzewski, the Russian revolutionist, who wrote a pamphlet on this matter. George Jacob Holyoake was judiciously to the front as usual, and his brother, Austin, and to assist the cause brought forth a series "Tyranicide literature" commencing with an edition of "Killing no Murder," by Col. Titus. This was followed by a poem by Percy Greg, which if I understand the English language, was a direct instigation to assassination, and remarkable for the prophecy it contains of the fate of the Napoleonic dynasty.

I confess to having had a deadly hatred to Louis Napoleon. Napoleon the Third, or "Little," as Victor Hugo christened him, for his betrayal of the French Republic. I was instinctively impressed with the belief that he was no friend to England, and I hated him also for the bad character he bore. His card sharping practices, his role as a bully, his swindling, his purjury. His successes only made me hate him the more. It was this hatred that caused me to write his life, a penny pamphlet, it is true ; but a pamphlet that did its work by its extensive sale. With many others, I was content to obey Landor's advice to watch and wait. I am free to admit that I gloried in his son's death, knowing full well his intention in setting foot on the African shore was to place himself in a position to create a disturbance in France, upset the republic, and place himself in his father's position. In his death, I saw peace, not for France alone ; but for the entire world. I knew well that there was not a drain of Napoleon's blood in his father's or his own veins—indeed that they were frauds, not that I should have respected them more had they been linked to the great Napoleon, whose memory to me is little less than a hideous nightmare.

In politics, however active things may be upon the surface, the events that startle the world, are due to the undercurrents. When Edmund Burke, the orator and statesman, returned from France on the eve of its greatest revolution, be pictured everything colour-de-rose, but "the inspired idiot," Oliver Goldsmith, saw matters in a different light, and asserted that she was on the eve of a revolution. The vision of Burke penetrated no farther than the surface, Goldsmith realised the strong undercurrent—the deep antagonism germinated in the minds of all Frenchmen against the then order of things. I have heard a friend of mine, from personal knowledge, describe the quietude that reigned in Hayti on the eve of its great earthquake. No one prophecied the impending calamity. The water girls with their pitchers went singing through its streets, without a thought of danger, and a calm quiet enveloped the city. No one vision penetrated below the surface. A similar state of things prevailed in Paris previous to 1792, when the author of the "Deserted Village" left France with his flute. The opinion of Burke was shared by the entire world, or nearly so. It is only given to few to see below the surface. As the compression of gunpowder makes it the more destructive so it is with a people's stifled hatred. Those who danced at the Tuilleries during Napoleon the Third's regime, knew nothing of the suppressed hatred and stifled wrath that threatened them.

I owe my introduction to William Morris to my friend, Trant, whom I first knew as the Secretary to Sir Charles Dilke. After leaving Sir Charles, Trant turned journalist, and I believe acted as war correspondent for one or more London newspapers. It was arranged that, on a given Sunday, that Trant and myself should proceed to the poet's home, on the Mall, Hammersmith. There is an old saying that "man proposes and fate disposes," and so it turned out with regard to the fulfilment of this arrangement. Before the day arrived, I was stricken with gout, and, in consequence, the engagement had to be set aside. The result of a sort of carte blanc that I should call whenever convenient to myself, and an intimation that a hearty welcome awaited me. On my recovery, I became aware of the fact that Mr. Morris would lecture at the Hall on his own ground on Socialism on a stated Sunday evening, and forthwith I determined to present myself on the occasion. I rang the bell about four at noon, announced my name and was invited to step into the library. I there, for the first time, saw the author of "John Ball." I found him to be a man built on very much the same lines as myself, of medium height and full habit of body. He was in harness, if I mistake not, engaged in the completion of his succeeding work. "Do you smoke, Leno?" were his first words, after the usual greeting. I replied "No; but I snuff." "Then have a pinch with me," was the rejoinder. After a few moments had elapsed, the conversation lapsed into a subject dear to both of us, namely, modern poets and modern poetry. Towards that conversation, I am afraid my contribution was of little value, still, I am bound to say that it was listened to with the greatest attention. Then followed an interchange of opinions on Owen and Socialist leaders of a half century back, and on the topic I had the advantage of a personal acquaintance with those who occupied the most prominent position. "I lecture this evening, and trust you can be present. If so, we will adjourn for tea." I signified my willingness, and after a glance through the contents of his book case which I found to contain an excellent assortment of books. On entering the dining room, I was introduced to his daughter, and a few other friends whose names have escaped my memory. A lively conversation ensued, and by the time the meal was concluded, the hour for the lecture arrived. Earnestness of purpose, a charming frankness, and free and easy style, to which may be added depth of thought, were its chief charms. At its conclusion, I was asked to say a few words. On the dismissal of the audience we returned to the dining room and found supper awaiting. I cannot avoid the opportunity of recording the delightful impression it made on me. I had never seen a home to compare with this for comfort and homeliness, nor met with a reception that gave me greater pleasure. But alas, I had to hurry away, for "time and trains wait for no man," says the proverb; but that is a mistake, for did not a Great Western train wait for the Shah of Persia, and did not my son-in-law lose a rich legacy from an aged aunt through waking her from her slumbers at midnight, in consequence of the succeeding train being started three hours later than usual? I thank Mr. Morris and his daughter for this oasis in the desert of an old man's life, for the break in the monotony of the evil times on which I have fallen, and I thank Mr. Morris for the boundless delight the presentation of his works has afforded me. May my poor efforts as a writer afford him half the pleasure I have derived from his. From words spoken, I could gather that he was not ignorant of their existence, and the republication in the "Commonweal," rightly or wrongly, impressed upon me the belief that, despite of their crudeness, he did not consider them worthless.

On Sunday evening, March 16th, 1890, I had been informed that a social gathering would take place in the small hall at the back of the publishing office of the "Commonweal" in Great Queen Street, London. I passed in by the side entrance to find I had been misinformed, and that, instead of an entertainment of the kind named, a purely business meeting in connection with the above socialistic newspaper was in progress. I was preparing to beat a retreat, which, was observed by Mr. William Morris. Rising from his seat, while shaking me warmly by the hand, he said "You need not go; we don't mind you, Leno, we have no secrets we desire to keep." After "exchanging a pinch of snuff," for we are a pair of snuffers, I reseated myself. The "Commonweal" is the acknowledged organ of one of the several organizations started for the spreading of socialistic views, and winning over recruits. The risk of its publication rests upon the shoulders of the poet of the Mall, and, moreover, the risks of fines and imprisonment for aught punishable that may appear in its columns. I soon learned that Mr. Morris occupied a position strangely similar to that I once held with regard to the "Commmonwealth." Money-finder, responsible head, and chief writer to what is commonly known as a working-class paper. Experience taught me to pity him. Yes, the "Commonweal" and the "Commonwealth" were, apparently, worked on the same lines, that is with a consulting committee, a multitude of advisers, and each committee man or adviser, fully impressed with a belief that he could do the work much better than it was being done. Plenty of adverse criticism, plenty of advice, and small aid, if any, to meet the cost of production, and other incidental expences. After listening to their carpings for a considerable time, Mr. Morris admitted the justness of a few of the views expressed, put his foot down on others, and plainly pointed out the position in which he was placed, and ended by expressing his willingness to hand over the paper and its entire management to them, so soon as they were in a position to take upon their shoulders the responsibilities that rested upon himself. All this was tempered by the kindliest-feeling and a manliness that, from my short acquaintance, is characteristic of the author of "John Ball." Should it get abroad that he is to be deposed or is deposed as the responsible head of the "Commonweal," will one of the carpers commit a like blunder that was made by a prototype, or parasite that attached himself to the "Commonwealth ?" A week or so too early, for his critical accumen it was my lot to run up against him. Holding out his hand, he commenced congratulating me on the improvement in the articles in the then current number of the paper. Seeing the mistake into which he had fallen, I pretended to agree with him. Then he was induced to mention the special articles which gave him such an impression. Just as I anticipated, he mentioned the leaders I had written. I immediately informed him of his error, that I was still editor, and that both the articles specified had been written by me. This self-appointed critic plainly exhibited his discomfiture, and after a laugh that I could not, and had no desire to suppress, we parted never to meet again. There are so many asses desirous of jumping into lions' skins, that I should not be surprised to see one squeezed into that of this great lion of literature, that is with his permission, in order to give him the chance of airing his vanity.

In my long term of life, I have had but one strong desir

and that has been justice and freedom to all mankind. I always asserted my right to think, speak and act, the latter with this proviso, that it should be to the wrongful injury of none. My religion has been morality and so it remains, and will so, I trust to the end. I have recognised the good of all religions, and equally condemned the priestcraft of all, and the hypocrisy of their professors. There are questions in theology that I have vainly tried to solve, and those who professed to be able to explain them, failed to give me satisfaction. In this uncertainty I was content to live, and am content to die. I was happy in it, and the man who thinks that an impossibility, is, I feel assured, akin to Dogberry, for what thought can be more consoling than that you have avoided doing injury to others, striven your best to uplift them, and striven to act out your thoughts, in other words, the determinings of your thoughts. You are endowed with the power of thinking—what for? I ask, if you are not sensitive to the importance of obeying the conclusions to which they lead you? Whatever punishment may be in store for me, it will not be for taking this course, and it will go hard with mortals who have done this if the stereotpyed belief in this should prove true.

I am now sixty-five, and I have many reminders that I am getting old. It is no use to lament now, one by one, my capacities and acquirements are surely leaving me. The first that took its department was my voice and power to use it to give joy to others. To how many circles of friends did this give me an introduction? In the country and in this great city, whereever I went, I soon found friends and a hearty welcome. Indeed, on more than one occasion, my merits as a singer found me bread when it was sadly wanted, and once brought me the offer of a living. I would not trust to it for a living; but the many good causes and good men I have been able to help when, without it, I must have acted like the Levite and left them to perish. The last request of Mrs. George Wheeler was that I should sing her a song by her sick bed. I attribute much of the extreme happiness I enjoyed in Dunstable, Windsor, and London, to my capacity to sing a song, which if not strictly artistic, was, like that of the wild bird, sweet and pleasing to the ears of my listeners.

I was never desirous to hear either of the songs I had written sung in the streets; but like the late Lord Houghton, I confess to the pleasure I received when I did hear them sung. I have and still hold to the opinion that the surest way to kill a good song is to over popularise it. "The Song of the Spade," and "Judge not a Man," are the only two songs I remember to have heard from the lips of a street singer. I should have been more pleased, however, if the singer had learned them from copies I had sanctioned. The alterations, I could plainly see, had been made to escape the penalties attached to the law of copyrights.

"Do you think, Leno," said Ernest Jones to me, as we were seated in Tom's Coffee House, in Holborn, "that a writer of lyrics can ever acquire a big reputation?"

"Why not," I replied.

"I think," was his reply, "that Burns has destroyed the chance."

I contented myself with pointing out that Tennyson's most successful efforts were of the lyrical order.

"The Song of the Spade" has been published in most European languages, and to at least four different tunes, in England and America, and proclaimed by no less an authority than the "Athenæum" as one of the best songs we possess, and gave me the title of the "Burns of Labour."

For the latter portion of my life, I have been forced to apply myself to purely local advocacy, and inasmuch as that is only of local interest, I will not trouble my readers further.

As an active member of the respective committees I helped to organize endless demonstrations including that to welcome Garibaldi, that held on Shakspeare's tercentenary, that in favour of Reform at Brompton, at the Agricaltural Hall, Islington, the burial of OConnor, George Odger, &c.

In addition, whenever it was thought advisable to send deputations on questions affecting the working classes, I was generally chosen. In that capacity, I have met with Palmerston,

Disraeli, Derby, Gladstone, &c., and, before the latter, it was my special duty to point out the unfairness of a two year residential qualification. This resulted in one year being made the qualifying period.

OPINIONS OF THE PRESS OF "DRURY LANE LYRICS."

"It is so seldom that books of poems are worth reading, especially when the author publishes them himself, that we are pleased to have the opportunity of perusing the collection of Mr. John Bedford Leno. His poetry is not mere rhyme; he posesses a poetic nature, and his modest preface enhances the value of the book, and shews the true stamp of merit."—THE WEEKLY TIMES, Jan. 5th, 1868.

"Mr. Leno is a working man to the backbone. He believes in the honour and dignity of labour, and sings while he toils in a right royal spirit. He is a Radical, but a poetic Radical, which is being a Radical with a difference. His songs are the genuine utterance of his own feelings and convictions, and out of the fullness of the heart his mouth speaketh. His place of residence has doubtless suggested the title of his volume, and it is not a bad one; for, inasmuch as Drury Lane is crowded with a teeming population of workers, and strugglers for bread in the battle of life, and his songs are, for the most part, on labour and struggling, and suffering, they bear their quaint title appropriately enough. Mr. Leno, like all other poets, loves the country. A breath of fresh air in the green fields, a ramble over a bit of wild moor land, or a stroll down a wild flower-decked lane, is a joy to his heart. A butterfly in the city will draw a song from him full of memories of the pleasant places whence the fragile but beautiful wanderer had come."—The BIRMINGHAM DAILY GAZETTE, Jan. 9th, 1868.

DRURY LANE LYRICS show keen relish for eternal beauty and deep sympathy with human nature under various conditions." ATHENÆUM, Mar. 28th, 1868.

Mr. Leno is a working man and sings buoyantly of labour. We fear, however, the fact of his being a daily toiler for his bread will be sufficient to earn for him the contempt of a few snarling and caddish pedants. That impotence and impudence are too often exhibited by scribblers of humble origin cannot be denied, and we have unfortunately among us a literary canaille grossness and feebleness. But we have brilliant exceptions among the lowly-born, who, without the aid of Oxford or Cambridge tutoring, have memorably enriched and beautified our literature. They have not drawn their inspiration from stout countesses and buxom barmaids, and consequently have not sickened us with erotic ravings. This meritorious volume deserves the patronage of all lovers of healthy patriotic lays."—PUBLIC OPINION.

"Mr. Leno's "Lyrics" are on the side of labour and strugling humanity, and will serve in no small degree to cheer the working man. From the ninty-five lyrics which make up his interesting collection, our space confines us to a few specimens. Let not our readers imagine that these are the gems of the volume: there are many much superior throughout the work which proclaim in tones of genuine melody the true dignity of labour. The book would be an ornament to any drawing-room table."—FALMOUTH AND PENRYN WEEKLY TIMES, Jan 11th, 1868.

The author, John Bedford Leno, as a poet, has been recognised and honoured by the elite of the working classes, still we believe that we are correct in saying that up to the period of our writing there has been no opportunity offered of obtaining anything approaching to a collection of his numerous poems.

At the termination of the engagement with Eliza Cook, the conductors of the WEEKLY DISPATCH filled the hiatus by publishing many of his well-known songs, including his most popular "Song of the Spade."

We are not surprised that so spirit-stirring a song should find a home on the other side of the Atlantic; indeed, it is as well-known there as in the author's native land. We may here add that the Chevalier de Chatelaine, the able French translator of Chaucer and Shakspeare, has not deemed this song of Mr. Leno's beneath his dignity; for he has rendered it familiar to his countrymen in a translation of uncommon excellence.

Mr. Leno is, beyond all question, the poet of the poor. His language consists of the choicest Saxon, and his thoughts are the every day thoughts of the great mass of his countrymen, sublimated by a rich and vigorous fancy. He is the very antithesis of the modern poet, and as such, objects to the use of all glitter and tinsel. What Ebenezer Elliott was to the principles of Free Trade in Corn, John Bedford Leno is to the more enduring theme of Labour—Equally strong, plain, and uncompromising.

Mr. Leno's feelings in this direction are well expressed in a poem, entitled a "Crowded Court."

In early life our author was associated with Gerald Massey in the production of the SPIRIT OF FREEDOM," a publication noted for its rigourous and untiring determination to call a "man a man, and a spade a spade." Unlike his friend Massey, Mr. Leno has adhered to his trade—that of a printer—and the cause he embraced in his early youth, and for the past twenty years has laboured continuously and unswervingly in the political redemption of the toiler. His first act after the passing of the Reform Bill, to the obtainment of which his labours largely tended, has been to issue the volume of which we are now speaking.

Nor is it as the poet of labour alone that we have praise to award; Mr. Leno has given ample proof in the volume before us that he can touch on gentle themes.—WOOLWICH GAZETTE, Jan. 18th, 1868.

A TALE OF SEVERN SIDE.

On Severn side, a mansion old
Looked out upon a barren wold !
A cheerless view, whose counterpart
Was in its owner's barren heart.
Its walls had chinks and crannies too,
And prying rays came glittering through,
And struggled—died amid the gloom
That reigned within each prison room.
Each door had more than usual guard,
A lock of many a curious ward,
Two ponderous bolts, beside a chain
That stretched across and back again.
The ample porch had given way
Beneath a niggard's unkind sway,
And left revealed the guarded door
To frown upon the passing poor.
Alas ! the charitable porch
Has passed from cottage, homestead, church,
And poverty now seeks a home
Beneath yon cold, forbidding dome,
Where man and woman, desolate,
May die without its guarded gate.
Oh ! what are tales of human woe
And Hunger, man's eternal foe,
But meaningless and empty words
That wake no echoes, touch no chords—
To those who crave for wealth untold,
And lose their hearts 'mid heaps of gold,
With souls that have no human tie,
By wealth reduced to beggary ?
A long and uncontrolled desire
All actions guide—all thoughts inspire,
And e'en success availeth nought,
There's poison in the golden draught
That leaves a burning thirst behind
That parches and consumes the mind.
When honoured Labour's task is done,
No barren comfort comes alone,
But joys unnumbered, numberless,
Each thought an angel sent to bless.
The miser lived, bowed down by care,
With features callous and austere,
With outward form quite shrunk and thin,
From want of blameless joy within ;
For no inspiring current ran
Within that cold and cheerless man ;
His scanty, meagre, threadworn dress,
Bespoke his rich and mean distress.

'Twas thus he might have sickened, died,
Had not an angel stood beside,
Of his scant joys, the only bringer,
Whose graceful, thin, white, tapering finger
Would oft direct his eyes to God
And plead with his own flesh and blood
Through Mary and her child. The cold
And false philosophy of gold
Knew no such God . . . . .
That prayer came through a mother's tongue,
The God-taught teacher of the young ;
She learned it by he mother's side :
The teaching lived, the teacher died.
'Twas long since Death her form despoiled,
Her spirit refuged in her child,
A child so fair, so meek withal,
Yet doomed to drink the dregs of gall
In life's probationary years,
And win her womanhood through tears.
Year followed year, but doomed to die,
And leave its heir a legacy
Of untold woes : still, that frail form,
(A lily in a world of storm)
Bore up, as those alone can bear
Who foster faith first won by prayer !
It seemeth strange that one so cold,
So fondly wedded unto gold,
Should be so blest ; but all is strange,
And who would seek God's will to change ?
It needs a deal of craft and stealth
To safely store a miser's wealth ;
But more of both, by far, I ween,
To watch and guard a virgin queen
Whose matchless beauty is a prize
Worth any human sacrifice.
Was ever maid with beauteous face
Secure in any hiding place !
Are Eastern harems all secure
Though eunuchs may be hard to lure,
And jealous eyes continual move
To mark the tortuous ways of love ?
Is there a spot beneath the sun
That human eye e'er rested on,
But what could tell of some fair maid
Whose guardian angel was betrayed,

Though doors were closed and windows barred,
And fancied safe by watch and ward?
An eye is turned, a staple gone—
And, lo! the watcher's left alone!
How slow and sad the moments pass
To those who sip from Sorrow's glass,
When grief bedims the youthful eye,
And clouds the fair-set memory;
But, slower still, if loneliness
Sits brooding o'er the heart's distress,
Counting the sands as, one by one,
They check the progress of the sun.
It was a glorious summer eve
When vagrant fancies deign to leave
A poet's brain; a time when love
Meets love; a time when brake and grove
O'erflow with richest song, and round
The humblest hearths blythe hearts are found.
Alone and cheerless, Mary sat
Watching the windings of a bat,
Whose very joy seemed mockery;
Alas! she wished she were as free
As that strange bird, or mouse, or both;
Hers was a drear, imprisoned youth
That knew no change. She looked around,
And, to discomfort, saw no bound.
A hopeless woe—a black despair—
Enthralled her breast with anxious fear.
Had heaven but sent a drooping dove
Careering o'er wild waves of love,
And bringing tidings as of old
From o'er the troubled waters cold,
Her breast had been an ark of peace.
She saw the living light decrease,
And dim grey clouds climb up the sky,
Where wise men read their destiny,
The fleet and airy steeds of even
Chasing the day athwart the heaven.
All quiet—scarce a zephyr stirred—
Save those that poised th' unfeathered bird;
Black clouds came hurrying to and fro,
And denser shades were spread below;
'Till earth was like some happy home
Where, uninvited, Death had come:
A moment since and all was fair,
And now 'twas darkness everywhere:
The sky a huge and dismal pall
That shut out light and shrouded all.

Nought could be seen—nor man nor beast;
The sky appeared as one vast waste
Of troubled waters—threatening death
To every breathing thing beneath.
Unwittingly her sire would roam
Beyond the limits of his home,
And seldom could he ever find
Aught so engaging to his mind
As casting up his golden store,
And longing—wishing it were more,
Or framing hidden traps for those
Whose riches would increase his woes.
'Twas thus he wandered—never heeding
How startled rooks were homeward speeding,
How skipping lambs had ceased to play,
And robin left the topmost spray;
Nor looked he at the changing sky,
For misers seldom look so high!
The pointed arch, the vaulted roof,
Is not the sole, convincing proof
Of gothic mould; the best is rude,
Symbolic of the multitude.
So Ruskin says, at least, no more,
Nor this could I stand voucher for;
But I have been in holy places,
Where grinning, scowling, ghastly faces
Reminded one of hell—forsooth!
The very thought makes me uncouth.
And I have sat within the aisles,
Of one at least of these strange piles,
And conjured devils---till I heard
The noise of chains when rudely stirred.
Her father passed as most devout
Of men---no Sabhath came without
His strict attendance on the priest,
Where, every minor sin confessed,
He stood by absolution free
From all the crimes of usury.
And Mary by his side would go
And tell her sins with heart of woe;
They were not great ones, to be sure,
For few, if any, were so pure.
She once confessed that she had heard
The priest give mass and that each word
Had passed unheeded---that her eyes,
Transfixed by Love's sweet sympathies,
Saw not the frowning faces round,—
She heard no more the rapturous sound
Of holy music—but that one,
As fair as eye e'er feasted on,

Stood by her side, and then she'd tell
How, led by love, by love she fell.
Ye maidens fair, who oft have strove,
To make the right supreme o'er love,
How often hath fair innocence
Acknowledged love's omnipotence!
A clouded brow---a stern control,
Embittered speech, and envious soul,
Fail to estrange a daughter's love,
That each unkindness tends to prove;
For woman's love will often cling
And breathe its last in worshipping
A heart unworthy of its zeal,
Whose sense of wrong, and power to feel
Her wise persuasiveness has gone. . . .
The ivy of the ruined stem
Is woman's love—and scar and seam
Are buried from the stranger's eye
In its mysterious sympathy.
As Mary listened in the lull
Of that wild storm—her heart so full
Of anxious grief—a crimson glow
Came mantling over cheek and brow;
A glow no mortal could create,
Nor wildest storm e'er penetrate.
It seemed to clothe her fragile form
In heaven's own armour, and the storm
Rushed howling by—and, big with ire,
Spoke words of wrath with tongue of fire.
Anon, this furious onslaught ends
Of more than twice five hundred fiends,
Leaving a terror in the air
That filled the sternest heart with fear.
The wild shriek of some unknown tongue,
Made shrill by pain, by terror strong,
Came, followed by the fearful cry
Of souls that war with agony.
That wild shriek was the onset blast,
For suddenly the sky o'ercast
Was pierced with lightning through and
  through.
But all the blasts that heaven could
  blow,
And all its anger cast below,
Could never make her soul despair,
While Faith and Love stood warders
  there.
She rushes to the Severn side,
And still, borne onward by the tide,
She hears the cry, and follows fast—
Ay, swifter than the swiftest blast;
Quick as the lightning flash she drew
The scarf from off her neck—and threw

It streaming o'er the wave—the wind,
Tempestuous in its wrath, proved kind,
And bore it to the outstretched hand.
. . . .
A monkish hood is frail disguise
To cozen Love's all-seeing eyes,
And though a death-fraught struggle may
Dash many a lineament away,
Through wreck, alone, we recognize
A cherished form—a face we prize,
And Mary saw, though changed by care,
A lover's features linger there.
Nor hand could paint, nor tongue could
  speak,
The crimson blush that lit her cheek;
It came like sunshine 'tween the rain,
And fled as angels fly again.
How hard are man's decrees to bear!
Though framed by monarchs, wise and
  dear,
They're seldom kept: those parents
  make,
Are vainly made—and sure to break.
Her father erred; he could but err,
In framing statutes stern for her,
For love that never knew a law,
Or, if it did, soon found a flaw.
The threshold's passed; beneath his roof
A lover sits—oh! stern reproof
To those grown old, who fain would try
To make one huge monopoly
Of those God's kindness sends to bless,
And fructify a wilderness.
As Draco's stern, tyrannic code
Gave way to sterner flesh and blood,
So perished his—so perish all
That hold the human heart in thrall.
Thus Love exists through endless gloom,
And, crucified, still braves the tomb,
Deathless as Christ, and ever young,
Strengthening as it suffers wrong,
Awaiting till that morn appears,
When it shall blossom void of fears,
And play on earth the angel-part
Of strengthener of the human heart,—
The ever-glorious, God-like role
Of purifier of the soul.
I fain would tell what lovers feel
For lovers' woes; how troubles heal
When touched by Love; what magic
  lies
In purely, heavenly, sympathies:
And prove by deeds that Mary did
What latent virtues may lie hid

In woman's soul : but, better far,
I'd tell how, like a living star,
She, restless, paced that dreary wild,
And angels high looked down and smiled ;
How she would lift her eyes above
And plead with all a maiden's love
For heaven to hold him perilless :
Then bade the raging storm confess
Him harmless. Pure and undefiled,
The noblest being 's but a child.
Alas, 'twas vain, no human prayer
Could stay the raging storm's career.
Far, far removed from mortal aid
The miser, stricken and dismayed,
Sinks friendless, shelterless, and weak,
Where threat'ning clouds in anger break.
How little is there left of man
As thus he lieth, cold and wan,
And motionless ; the reed that bowed
Its fragile head before the cloud
Now stands erect. Thus courtiers bow,
And raise themselves by bending low.
Oh ! God ! what are we at the best
But clay-built figures, slightly dressed
In seeming consciousness, and e'er
Controlled by pride, or ruled by fear.
Vain our ambition, vain our power,
They pass away in one short hour ;
While lifeless stones for ages tell
When men are tongueless, how they fell !
'Twas not the miser's worshipped gold
That heard his shouts across the wold.
Vain man, thou canst not in thy pride
The living laws of God deride
Unchecked—thou canst not ruthless sit
Triumphant on thy throne of wit ;
For He so wills that every soul
Is subject to his fixed control ;
And though, perchance, we may not see
The strength that lives in this decree,
Yet each has felt its wondrous force,
And, feeling, failed to stay its course.
Winged hope o'ertaketh dull despair,
The leaden curse gives way to prayer,
While prayers, like exhalations, rise
To add new glory to the skies.
When man is stricken by disease,
When cruel 'plaints his body seize,
Who but fair woman can he find
To tend his wants, and soothe his mind ?
Her silvery tones fall like a shower
Upon a parched and withered flower :
Her watchful eye and winning smile,
Her meekness, love, (untouched by guile)
Like sunshine, enter on the soul,
And with a mild, yet firm control,
Unbind Death's icy, chilling hand,
And bid our numbered days expand.
A shepherd's wife—a comely dame,
Whose modest worth deserved a fame
Enduring as the skies above,
Welcomed, with pity and with love,
The miser to her humble hearth,
And proved how thoughtfulness from dearth
May lovingly provide and bless
The poorest home with happiness.
The simplest flower in desert lands
Claims more respect, more love commands,
Than all the flowers on earth beside,
With all their splendour and their pride.
Deserted and devoid of care,
It speaks of God to wanderers there,
And shows how humbleness may give
What riches cannot—that we live
To bless the earth, and none so low
Who cannot something still bestow
To cheer the weary and the worn,
And still the breast by trouble torn.
Ye dwellers 'neath the northern skies
Who eastward cast your longing eyes,
And bless the sun who scatters gold
Upon your hostile regions cold,—
Should e'er that sun adventure forth
Upon the desolated north,
And, with a miser's crafty stealth,
Withhold his boundless light and wealth,
Who, then, will bless and welcome give,
The starved his bounty should relieve,
The perishing his gold might save
From poverty, despair, and grave ?
What envious son of womankind,
With callous heart and selfish mind,
Shall glory seek in endless wealth,
Obtained by treachery and stealth,
While others battle with distress,
Or wander in a wilderness
Of woe, and breathe an endless sigh,
With no returning sympathy.
The morning came, and by his side
With anxious eye, the peasant bride

Still watching sat—no power could move,
Or woo her from her task of love.
Strange dreams disturbed his fitful rest,
And stranger things these dreams confessed:
They tell how love of gold destroys
All virtuous hopes and heavenly joys,
How breaks asunder tenderest ties,
And rends the dearest sympathies,
And makes the weak and timid bold
In crime, if crime but purchase gold;
They tell how misers win their store,
And, winning, coin their souls for more,
Forgetful of the laws which bind
E'en misers to their fellow kind.
Anon, they tell of days bygone,
When, as a youth, he stood alone
On life's broad highway, had not Care,
Fast following, claimed acquaintance there;
How friends arose, and fortune smiled
Upon a poor, down-trodden child;
How pride grew in his humble breast,
And dreams of love disturbed his rest;
Of nuptial joys, and death's fell power
To blast all hope in one short hour.
He, weeping, wakes, the spell has gone,
And dull remembrance reigns alone.
The careful dame stood watchful by,
With more than woman's sympathy.
"Be calm," she said, "dispel thy fears,
And rob not children of their tears;
Thy daughter comes, and here thou'lt find
None, save the honest and the kind."
The timid stars came peering forth
To guide the children of the earth
O'er unknown seas and pathless moors,
O'er desert tracks on desert shores,
As Mary bade her love adieu,
Her breast disturbed by passions new.
Many a wreck strewn o'er the scene
Now pointed where the storm had been,
And how heaven's warriors scathless ride
While scattering ruin far and wide.
A sense of loneliness and fear
Came o'er the maid, as, cold and drear,
She sat and wept! she knew not why
The tears came rushing to her eye.
She felt as one who dimly sees
A future filled with miseries;
Or one who unknown paths have trod
And wondered if they led to God!

A letter bore the bitter truth
To her whose long-imprisoned youth
Had but increased her power to feel
The force of Sorrow's barbèd steel.
When dangers lurk round those we love,
No earthly power can e'er remove
The rising doubts that fill the mind:
E'en honied words leave stings behind.
But, friends, alas! she had not one,
Her only friend to heaven had gone
Ere she could plainly speak her name,
And oft she wondered why she came
Into a world so desolate,
Where none save angels knew her fate.
With troubled heart she took her way
To where her stricken father lay:
She bathed his aged face in tears,
And, smiling, chased away his fears;
Then showered sweet kisses on his brow,
And smoothed his scanty locks of snow;
Bade him be cheerful with his lot,
And, like an angel, filled the cot
With blessings new—her virtues rare
Shed rays of sunshine everywhere.
A month passed by ere he could leave
The only couch the poor could give,
And thousands were the thanks she gave
To those who stretched their hands to save.

Once more on Severn's side they dwell,
Once more they see its waters swell,
While autumn winds rush shrieking past,
And red leaves ride upon the blast.
The frame diseased may wear away,
Within the grasp of fell decay,
And yet the mind grow strong and free
T'unmask the loathsome subtlety
That binds our healthful life within
The deadly coil of hateful sin.
'Twas thus, amid the throes of pain,
She saw, with loathing and disdain,
The niggard joys of wealth, and sought
With deeply penetrating thought,
The source of joys more deep, and found
They sprang from higher, holier ground.
And, now, no more he treats with scorn
The humble and the lowly born,
Nor, envious, views the rich and gay,
Who live to lounge on life's highway.
The winter groweth old, and spring
Leaps forth a wayward scatterling;
But, rich anon, a thousand bowers
It mantles with the choicest flowers.

No more shall love of gold disarm
Fair Nature of her every charm.
He wanders forth at early dawn
O'er spangled lea and scented lawn,
And Mary by his side is seen
As smiling as a May-day queen;
Plucking a garland for her sire,
And meeting every half desire.
The winter breaking into spring,
And bidding every mute bird sing,
Brought less of joy to Mary's mind,
And had more sorrow intertwined,
Than this new season of the soul
That o'er her parent calmly stole.
Each cotter's child knew Mary's tread,
Each sire called blessings on her head,
Each matron's heart, in gratitude,
Cherished the spot where Mary stood.
With love-lit eyes she sees the change,
And oft in secret would she range
The cherished thoughts she hid within
Her guileless heart, as though 'twas sin
To love and be beloved. Her tongue
Stood motionless, as though a wrong
Were waiting to condemn her soul.

. . . .

'Tis thus the tongue should play the part
Of sentinel of the human heart
Or brain—nor let such thoughts escape
'Till they are framed to virtue's shape.
Each lengthening day threw flowers around
The maiden's path, and soon she found
His stength restored. Her child-like wiles
Once slain by fears, now fed on smiles;
And yet, when she was happiest,
A look betrayed, a thought confessed
A mind disturbed; no joy can hide
A love entombed—a buried pride.
The master-thought looks through the face,
And stealeth or imparts a grace.
As moon and sun rule night and day,
The spirit ever moulds the clay.
By cunning words her father learnt
How hidden love more fiercely burnt,
And how youth's beauty dies away
Beneath its fierce, unfettered sway:
And when he heard whom Mary loved,
He wondered, blessed her, and approved.
A fairer day ne'er broke in light
Through the dark barriers of the night,
Nor are its glories doomed to fade
Ere earth has its vast circuit made.
The linnet and the speckled thrush
Are making love from every bush,
The redbreast, mated on the snow,
Sits singing on th' abandoned plough,
The bird that hath so often striven
(Frail messenger of earth and heaven)
To win a passport from the Lord
Is once more falling like a sword!
By outward gloom we've inward care,
By outward joy we joyous are;
Then, oh! what joy for her is born
Who greets it as her bridal morn!
Now, high above the saintly isles
Each sculptured face is wreathed in smiles,
Gay, undisputed smiles, that seem
To say the frowning past's a dream.
The priest, no lean-faced anchorite,
Is clothed in stole and surplice white!
His clerk a holy vessel bears
With water pure as angels' tears;
And he who long had stood between
A buried love that bloomed unseen,
With liberal hand, bestows a prize
That makes man's home a paradise.
The richest earthly gift's a bride
By love and doubt long purified,
And such alone was she who trod
The flooring of that house of God.
Their troth, life-pledged, the happy pair
With holy water sprinkled are;
The circle women prize the most
Is then with holy water crossed,
And, in the name of all the Three
That constitute the Trinity,
With love abounding everywhere,
The rite concludes with one short prayer:
Oh! God! who rules the earth and sky,
Give heed, we pray Thee, to our cry;
Be to thy handmaid kind and just,
And guard her from all venal lust;
That she may ever faithful prove
And lightly bear the yoke of love."

List to the bells, how loud they speak!
Beware! for hearts with joy oft break;
List to the bells! oh, save in dreams,
Whoever heard such wondrous streams
Of rich, rare tones? List to the bells!
Ye charmèd hills and raptured dells!

Oft have I heard the summer rain
Break forth in such another strain ;
Yet, milder far—how like the sweet
Prattle of children's tiny feet.
The human heart is passion's home,
There joy must live, ere joy can come,
And 'tis from out the ringers' hearts
Such sweet and heaven-like music starts ;
But not from ringers' hearts alone
Could come the joy that filled each tone,
Each friendly pulse that beat around
Was robbed t' enrich the thrilling sound,
Ay, robbed, as peasants robbed their bowers
To strew the homeward path with flowers.
So well had this pure maiden strove
To win a neighbouring people's love,
That many trudged o'er many miles
To make her marriage rich in smiles.
There is a power we call decay
That never slumbers night or day ;
Its victims are beneath our tread,
For sea and land are paved with dead :
It dwelleth with the hermit lone,
With silent steps it mounts the throne,
The ruddiest cheek in turn discloses
How snug 'twill lie concealed by roses.
A year had scarcely passed away,
When life's long, feeble, flickering ray
Forsook the bent and tottering frame
Of him who bravely outlived shame—
The miser who had learned in woe
The source from whence true comforts flow.
Should'st thou e'er chance to tread the aisle
Of that old, lingering, moss-clad pile
Where Mary looked and loved—thou'lt see
Inscribed in solid masonry,
His precious gifts to England's poor,
And, hard beside the western door,
The grave of her he loved—and there
The sculptured forms of angels fair
Outstretch their hands o'er Mary's tomb,
As though inviting her to come
Away, where clouds are broke and riven,
To grace the marvellous throne of heaven.

TALES OF ELD.

THE RUINED CASTLE.

he castle you see's over yonder—
   I don't know its history, sir,
But it stretches away to past ages,
   I've heerd it be ever so far.
It war built afor Holifer Crumble
   And Old Julia Cesar war born :
I can jest see the top of its towers,
   A-standin' above the ripe corn.

Look ! there it be, clearer and clearer,
   There's no one, sir, lives in it now;
There's lots of it gone into ruins,
   Bin ground into dust by the plough !
And the whole as be left be quite shaky,
   And, totterin', threatens to fall ;
It was built mighty strong, I dessay, sir,
   But Time plays the devil with all.

Oh, yes, it be covered with ivy,
   That's clambered right up to the top,
Ah, so it be, jest as you say, sir,
   A sort of a natteral prop ;
It don't mind the wind, not a bit, sir,
   Though it rocks like a cradle, I'm told,
For two thousand years, I have heerd, sir,
   It's weathered the frost and the cold.

There, now we're a leetle bit nearer,
   Jest look at them two bits o' towers,
With jassamine trailing all over,
   With bunches o' lily-white flowers ;
There, look at them, beant they quite pratty,
   Togged out in their white-spotted green ?
An' them 'ere American creepers
   A-hanging their blue lamps atween.

There's lots of it made into pig-stys,
   They uses it up as it falls,
An' big pieces, carved, sir, all over,
   Be stuck in them 'ere garden walls ;
It serves for all manner o' uses,
   I've seen 'em a cartin o' loads ;
It do, sir, it comes in quite handy
   For stoppin' up holes in the roads.

Yes, I s'pose it be all right and proper,
   It bean't fit to live in, that's clear ;
Old castles, old houses, old people,
   They've paved all the roads about here.
But let us get on to the castle,
   I likes them old ruins, I do,
They remind me how strong I was once, sir,
   And what I am fast coming to.

There, wouldn't it look well in a pictur',
   If white-washed a bit here and there ?
An' them old battered walls over yonder
   Was put in a state of repair ?
If they fitted new panes in them winders,
   And mended that arch that guv way,
And stopped up them walls there, afore us,
   With plenty of putty and clay.

As you say, sir, sich mendings might spoil it,
   It arn't for the such likes o' me
To say what to do wi' old castles,
   Or judge what a pictur should be ;
They be out o' my line, sir, be sich things,
   So don't mind a bit what I say ;
Still, I fancies if some one don't stop 'em,
   They'll cart that old ruin away.

"The dungeon?" ah! that's kivered over;
  No, thank yer, it wouldn't suit me;
It wur awfully dark, I be told, sir,
  An' water stood up to your knee.
Oh! yes, there were plenty who died there,
  Some hundreds, I've heerd tell, and more;
But here be a chap full o' stories,
  An'll spin yer strange yarns by the score.

Come, Jim, sit yer down, lad, beside us,
  This gemman was passin this way,
And he wants to find out 'bout the castle—
  I've told 'un all I've got to say.
Just spit him out one of them stories
  That you have so oftentimes told,
'Bout them chaps who got fightin for freedom,
  And died in the struggle of old.

—o—

JIM'S STORY.

The shades of night were falling over mead, and marsh, and moor,
Over widely scattered homesteads, over dwellings rich and poor;
And merry elves, and wicked sprites, and fairies fond and free,
Were gathering from near and far beneath the trysting tree.

Over yonder rugged mountain the pale-faced moon looked down,
The curfew-bell was ringing from the steeple of the town,
And moping owls who shun the light had started on the wing,
And the sleeping leaves of forest trees had ceased their whispering.

Steathily, stealthily, down yon lane that crosses the bridle way,
Over the meadows of steaming swathes of fragrant, new-mown hay;
Down by the stream meandering in the fertile vale below,
Where the daffodils in the merry spring-tide in the pride of beauty glow;

Fearfully, fearfully, one by one, in the darkness of the night,
In those dreary days that followed in the wake of Hastings' fight,
A score of Saxons sternly true, who had sworn to do or die,
Were hastening on to the cherished priest who ruled in the abbey hard by.

Oh! for a leader, brave and strong, to lead the southern men,
Like Hereward, bold Hereward, who guarded Lincoln fen;
The worthy son of the worthy dame who naked rode her steed,
To serve the people of Coventry in their bitter hour of need.

There was Sandy Ralph and Tim o'th' Wind, and the Netherd of Rottendeen,
And the minstrel bold who had borne the palm on the night of Halloween,
And Clem o' the Clough, and Will o' the Wisp, the Pedlar and Little John,
And the arrow-maker who dwelt in the croft in the hundred of Hillingdon!

"Bring out," cried the Abbott, "the wassail bowl, and drink, ye brave men all,
The toast I give is 'Our Saxon Rights, and the Bastard's swift downfall.'"
And oaths were sworn to light the land from 'the gleaming sword of the fen,'
And round and round the bowl was passed, and round and round again.

"A few bold spirits," cried Clem o' the Clough, "and the glorious deed is done!"
"Our Saxon brothers, prickt with wrong, will fight," cried Little John.
"There is never a man," said Sandy Ralph, "who owns a Saxon name,
Who will not rush to the battle field to share our deathless fame."

"The arrows I've made are tipped with steel, and fashioned straight and true,"
Said the maker who dwelt at Hillingdon croft, "and never will go askew."
And then upspoke brave Will o' the Wisp, the cunningest of them all,
Who swore to live till the fight was won, or with the foremost fall.

The minstrel bold was stringing o' rhymes
    the abbot was noting down,
And the serving man was toasting crabs
    for the rich ripe ale and brown,
When a crash was heard at the Abbey
    door and springing o' foot each said :
"Will you fight or fly? Will you live or
    die? since we have been betrayed?"

No answer came, but the flash of swords,
    and a wild and ringing cheer,
As the sound of the tramp of armèd men
    rang nearer and yet more near;
And hand to hand, and foot to foot, a
    deadly sight to see,
With might and main the Saxons fought
    the men of Normandie.

The stern old Abbot, with fiery zeal,
    though wounded, still pressed on,
And right and left, on either side, fought
    Clem and Little John,
And wounded sore, in crimson gore, a
    heap of foemen lay—
With battered skulls and bloody wounds
    on the flagstones cold and grey.

Will o' the Wisp, with stealthy tread, kept
    flitting here and there,
And through the chinks of fighting friends,
    like lightning shot his spear,
And the arrow-maker, perched on high,
    was plying his cross bow free,
And well in time, the man o' rhyme,
    fought fast and furiouslie.

Like brothers true, fought Sandy, Ralph
    and the Netherd of Rottendeen,
And higher and higher the corse pile rose
    of Norman foes between;
And the pedlar fairly to frenzy wrought,
    warred on with might and main,
And the cleaving force of his battle axe
    clove many a skull in twain.

But Norman still on Norman pressed, no
    breathing space had they,
And muscle will tire, and spirit will flag,
    and nerve at last give way;
And so it fell in that gallant strife, in the
    abbey that stood below,
'Ere that sturdy band of Saxon braves
    had met their overthrow.

The burly Abbot outspent at last, all
    faint from waste of blood,
And Clem o' the Clough, who fought by
    his side, who'd shock on shock withstood,
And Little John and Sandy Ralph, were
    flagging in the fray,
The whole front rank of the deathless
    few who had kept the foe at bay.

Will o' the Wisp, all prostrate stretched,
    on the blood-stained abbey floor,
And the arrow-maker's quiver spent, and
    the minstrel bathed in gore;
And the Netherd is breathing fast and
    low in the corner where he fell,
But the tale of the after butcheries is far
    too sad to tell.

If you'll come with me, now my story's
    done, to the edge of that dark pine
    wood,
I'll show you the traces of ruins still,
    where that bloodstained abbey stood,
"Now take a pull at the brandy flask."
    "Aye, willingly," say I,
For telling that story of old world deeds
    has left me parched and dry.

—o—

AFTER THE BATTLE OF HASTINGS.

Of those terrible times that followed fast
    on the day when Harold fell,
A Saxon bard, in mercy spared, in quaint
    old rhymes would tell:
And here is a tale that he used to sing in
    mild and bated breath,
In those dark, sad days when the Norman ruled, and the wage of singing
    was death.

It was after the fight was over, and the
    battle was fought and won,
When the pale-face moon was shining in
    the face of the crimson sun,
That a Saxon mother, whose son had
    fought in the thick of the fight that
    day,
Was scanning the corses, one by one, in
    the sadness of dismay.

THE AFTERMATH.

Like a spectre she moved o'er the battle-
 field, no thought of fear had she,
Her only care was her missing son in her
 pallid misery;
Of him she had loved with a mother's
 love, and watched with a mother's care;
Her lad with the large dark hazel eyes,
 and streaming nut-brown hair.

Over the hill, and down the dale, and
 athwart the corse-strewn plain,
She looked for him she had cherished
 long, and never would fondle again;
For, yonder, afar by the dark wood side,
 in the midst of a tangled brake,
Her only son lay stiff and cold, for good
 King Harold's sake.

In the dead of the night they buried him,
 in a trench by the dark wood side,
The widow's son, who had rose that morn
 in the flush of his strength and pride;
And over his body the cold earth lies,
 with never a stone to say
How he fought and fell for this dear old
 land on that thrice cursed, fatal day.

When the sun arose on the next day
 morn, the mother still journeyed on,
In the hope of finding among the dead,
 her darling, worshipped son;
Over the hill, and down the dell, by
 copse, and ditch, and lane,
Searching for him who will never move
 in the light of her love again.

The months roll by, and the spectre still
 is pacing the old, old round,
Though the harvest of death, long gathered in, is nowhere to be found;
Though friend and foe who fell asleep on
 that dark and treach'rous day,
Are resting together in endless peace in
 their winding sheets of clay.

Now, slower, and slower, and slower still,
 her weary round she goes,
Unmindful of rain, of hail, or sleet, and
 the angry wind that blows;
Unmindful of heat, of cold, or damp, no
 feeling or thought has she;
But a lingering hope that will never die,
 till death shall set her free.

Though her eyes are blind, she can picture still the form she will see no
 more,
Of the stalwart youth who grew from the
 babe she nourished in days of yore;
Of him whom she rocked in his earliest
 hours, and watched with the tenderest care,
When a helpless baby with hazel eyes and
 locks of nut-brown hair.

Down the valley and over the hill, and
 away through the beechen grove,
The spectre wanders and wanders on, in
 search of her widowed love;
Over the grave where he sleeping lies,
 unmindful of her who strays
In search of the idol she worshipped in
 those old post-nuptual days.

For many a month, for many a year, she
 paced her monotonous round,
Searching by day, and resting by night,
 on that famous battle ground;
Only a thought, only a wish, sufficing to
 urge her on,
Sleeping to dream that she clapsed him
 tight, and waking to find him
 gone.

But flesh and bone will waste away, and
 grief corrode the heart,
And clinging life will loosen its ties, and
 finally depart;
And so it fell, as the old rhymes tell, in
 the midst of storm and rain,
The mother was found on the clay-cold
 ground of that now historic plain.

When Jim's second story was ended,
 The gemman jest took a stroll round
To look at the site of the abbey,
 And glance at the castle and mound;
Then we showed him the way to the vil-
 lage
 That plays at "Bo-peep" in the vale,
And drank "Here's long life to yer ho-
 nour!"
 In tankards of village-brewed ale.

THE LAST BATTLE. (A.D. 2000.)

In wars of bygone ages, Freedom fought with fettered hands,
Against a host whose numbers were as countless as the sands;
She knew her sons were valiant; but, alas! it needed gods
To turn the tide of battle 'gainst such large and wond'rous odds.
She had her own Gethsemane of bloody sweat and tears,
And wore, alas! her crown of thorns and bore her cross in tears;
Her Judases betrayed her, and her watchers fell asleep,
And others swore they knew her not, with curses loud and deep!
She drank the bitterness of gall, and cried, in misery,
"Eloi, lama sabachthani," my God's forsaken me!
Clad in mail and bound together, all her foes came marching forth,
With the crushing force of icebergs in the seas that guard the north;
Or waves, lashed into fury by the rude, tempestuous wind,
Whose broken front reveals the power of forces ranged behind.
Half fed, half clad, disjointed, such, alas! was Freedom's host,
Her navy but a cockle shell, a thing to hug the coast;
Her arms, the instruments of peace, or weapons thrown away
As useless, worthless lumber, in the wars of yesterday.
Who wonders Freedom, beaten, roamed the world in strange disguise,
And hid in loathsome caverns from the reach of prying eyes?
Who wonders that she crouched in fear, and failed to trim Hope's lamp,
In living tomb, and darksome mine, in lonely, dismal swamp?
Who wonders that, to gather strength, she shunned the light of day,
To fight anew and conquer in the merry month of May.
The lark was carolling on high, soft waves caressed the shore,
And flowers, dyed in rainbow tints, sprang glittering to earth's floor;
While linnets, perched on hawthorn sprays, poured forth wild notes of love,
And robin, thrush, and song birds all, made music in the grove.
It was a May day morning, the merriest earth had seen,
Since tree and shrub, and hill and dale, put on their robes of green;
The hedgerows wore their richest gems of blossoms, white and red,
And the god of light, in a world of fire, was reigning overhead.
It was no time to dream of wrong, or carnage, born of hate,
For looking back, regretfully, on man's long lost estate;
But a time for merry beards to wag, for Joy to wear his crown,
To lift the nectared cup of life, and turn it upside down.
But all the harmony of birds, the merry hum of bees,
The glorious burst of blossoms, from flowers and from trees,
The shimmering light, the jewelled earth, the high-throned god of fire,
Could cure the rankling wounds of strife, and lift this old world higher.
The merriest day that earth e'er saw, will be remembered long,
For deeds of blood and bravery, that sprang from sense of wrong;
The last great fight of a doomèd race with men who would be free,
Where crownèd kings and mitred priests, went down in a crimson sea!
It was a May day morning, when the people's gathered chiefs
Determined to avenge their woes, and sweep away their griefs;
When wrongs that lived for ages, and wrought a world of woe,
Were calling for the sickle, for the reaper, and the blow!
In castles, strong and hoary, there were whispered words of fear,
And the clank of war's preparing notes burst on the startled ear;
In mansions built by plunder of nations lying waste,
The slaves in thought, and slaves in deed, were gathered in hot haste.
It was a May day morning, when the bandits of the world

Shook out their blood-stained banners,
and threats of vengeance hurled;
When the priest gave up his crozier for
the bright and dazzling sword,
Forgetful of the gentle life, the mission,
and the word.
Amid the golden splendour, the song of
bird and bee,
The tramp of feet, the driver's shout, and
blood-stained revelry;
Then blast of trumpet, beat of drum,
and voices hoarse and clear,
And now the shock of phalanxed men
bursts on the startled ear;
Then, over the hills and far away, the
loud-mouthed cannon roared,
And through each gorge that cleft the
hills an armèd host was poured;
While armies hid in coverts vast, and
sheltered in the den,
And heath and plain, and moorland wild,
were filled with panting men.
The helmet's plume, gay banneret, and
gold-bedizened flag,
Waved, side by side, in the full noontide,
with Glory's tattered rag;
And warlike chiefs, on distant hills, in
earnest council met,
Where the brazen cap of war usurped the
golden coronet.
Thick wreaths of smoke in branches hung,
and rose in mimic clouds,
And spread themselves like winding sheets
and white-edged funeral shrouds;
Or crept, as monsters crept of eld, amid
the heather bloom,
The spear-leaved grass, the spike-armed
furze, and golden bells of broom.
The men who'd wrought in iron for the
paltry bribe of pay,
And forged the mighty engines that held
all right at bay,
Had struck the work of tyrants, and, in
workshops near and far,
Were forging bolts of thunder for the
people's holy war.
And those who'd rifled regions where
infernal spirits dwell,
For earthquake force and prisoned death,
for tyrants, born of hell,
Were drawing down the lightning for the
victory of those
Who'd sworn, ere day had passed away,
to scatter Freedom's foes.

The blotted thoughts of thinkers, the
smothered words of men,
Like molten ore, ran, hissing hot, from
ransomed tongue and pen;
And poets who had sung of love and
knighted chivalry,
Attuned their harps anew and sang the
anthems of the free.
Men kissed their cradled babes in haste,
with teardrops in each eye,
And mothers choked with anguish, breathed that fatal word, " Good-bye!"
And white-haired parents gave their sons
to swell the list of braves,
And walked with tottering limbs, alone,
contented to their graves;
And gentle maidens kissed in tears, and
tore themselves away
From truant-hearted lovers, in the merry
month of May.
It was a May day morning, and this old
world gushed with life,
And daylight dreamers walked abroad
without a thought of strife;
'Till booming cannon shook the hills, and
smoke obscured the sky,
And the ear was rent asunder by the
shouts of victory!
The names of brave Leonidas and Curtius
arose,
And Hampden, Cromwell, Hofer, Tell,
were heard amid the blows;
And Hereward, and Winkelreid, and
names forgotten long,
Had the minstrels of the people failed to
cherish them in song.
And poets, dead, retouched their strings,
and fired the souls of men,
And flags, long rotting in the shade,
streamed in the wind again.
A miracle was wrought that day, and
graves gave up their dead,
And martyred hosts in council sat, and
martyred leaders led.
Unlike the puny wars of old, where each
man sought his foe,
And struggled hard, with might and main,
to work his overthrow;
When bended bow and pointed shaft, and
battle-axe and pike,
Was each, if wielded well, enough to
cause a foe to strike.
Now bursting shell and mitrailleuse, and
engines, new and strange,

Are ringing with the sound of death, from every mountain range !
Now sheeted flames spread o'er the land, and withered in a breath,
And Science, wedded unto Life, played concubine to Death ;
And curious vessels cleaved the sky, and hurled destruction round,
'Till corses piled on corses, rose, and, 'cumbered all the ground ;
Fell vapours, stifling beast and man, were rising from the plain,
And men in lusty life, who breathed, will never breathe again.
Athwart the sky, pace to and fro, strange shapes of floated things,
Of mimicked dragons, mimicked birds, that moved withouten wings,
And fiery flames of molten ore in one continuous flow,
Were falling, ever falling, blasting everything below.
On every mountain top that night a sacred light was burning,
And households gathered near and far to see their friends returning,
And muffled bells and bells of joy rang out from every steeple,
For grief that choked each widowed heart, and joy that filled the people.
And glad news spread like rays of light, and eyes made red with sorrow
Re-filled with joy, burned fiercely bright, to meet the gladsome morrow.

. . . . .

That morn, a little boy from school was keeping holiday,
And, as he roamed the meadows through, he gathered crimson may ;
And, thus he said to her beside, "What made the white may red?"
"They crowned the living Christ with thorns, " and nothing more was said.
"They crowned the living Christ with thorns," the words rang in his ear,
And, passing through his father's hall, he dropt the flowers in fear ;
And there they lay, at close of day, as red as red could be,
The crimson-dyed, from the crucified Godman of Gallilee !

A stateley dame passed through the hall and the burning lamp she bore,
Revealed the bunch of crimson flowers, the blood-stain on the floor,
And, staggering back, she shouted loud, "God's mercy ! is it so !
Then may, red may, the red-cross may, will hide the spotless snow.
Go ! bid the man of death prepare the trappings and the tomb,
The hatchment for the castle wall, the dark and sombre plume;
For all is lost ! the king is dead ! the populace hold sway !
The legend and the prophecy reveal themselves to-day !
Go ! bid them search the battle field—the corse-encumbered ground,
The bloodiest swathes that Death has reaped, till Leofric is found ;
And set the bells a-tolling loud in hamlets far and wide,
The king is dead ! the people live ! long live the crucified !
I loved the man, but not the king ; I love the people more,
I cease to be a Christian when I cease to love the poor ;
And, like to her of Coventry, who won immortal fame,
Would pluck out their redemption from the burning heat of shame.
I've read Christ's story o'er and o'er, 'tis in my memory now ;
I see the God-man on the cross, with thorns upon his brow ;
For Christ, I read the people ; for Lamb, the people shorn ;
For crown of thorns and heavy cross, the burthens they have borne ;
For resurrection and the life, I read the slave made free,
The grand apotheosis of long-martyred liberty.
I read how Christ, the crucified, had triumphed o'er the tomb,
And knew the resurrection, fair Freedom's day would come ;
I craved to see the better life, like sunshine come again—
The shackles falling from the slave—the rising up of men !

DIVINE RIGHT.

You've read of infants being changed by nurses in their cradles,
Of children born to wooden spoons and some to silver ladles;
Such tales are common, take my word, and never dare to doubt it;
But, if you fail, read my tale through, 'tis just as true without it.

Now list to me, and I will tell about a royal bab(b)y,
And one whose parents wore, I'm told, their toggery quite shabby;
The two extremes of wealth and want at distances bewilderin',
Were pictured to the perfect life in these contrary children.

Within a castle, old and strong, and guarded round with ramparts,
With waters dammed which neighbours called, quite properly, the damp parts;
A child was born, one summer morn, whose blood was all cerulian,
And christened, it was in July, appropriately Julian.

Another brat, another sprat, was spawned about this same time,
Another little July'un, (you'll please excuse this lame rhyme;)
And all the serving folks about, who toiled within the castle,
Declared they were as much alike as two peas from a parcel.

The weeks flew by, the months rolled on, and year on year came crawling,
Since these two kids, so much alike, announced their birth by squalling.
And now these youths are bosom friends, your doubts just please to smother,
The prince cared nought for pride of race, and each felt like a brother.

'Twas not in looks alone they paired, but in their separate natures;
In gait, in voice, the likeness was more perfect than in features;
In all their pleasures 'twas the same, in eating, fasting, drinking,
This sameness, like a ticking clock, kept evermore repeating.

From top to toe, in mind and soul, you couldn't tell one from t'other,
Yet each a different father had, and each a different mother;
They thought alike, they spoke alike, they loved the self-same weather,
And, like the Perreaus, had one forged, they would have forged together.

To keep these youths from getting mixed, as far as they were able,
They stuck upon the needy back an impecunious label,
And, on the richer, lower down, that part which tapers narrow,
Or lower still, for aught I know, they put the king's broad arrow.

While bathing in the pool one day, that pool I well remember,
A summer's day, in June or May, it might have been September,
The wetted labels, both fell off! oh! sore and sad disaster,
The arrow from the prince's back, and impecunious plaster!

Oh! woeful day! oh! sad mishap! oh! frightful misadventure!
For who can tell a royal swan, without a king's indenture?
And what wise man, in court or camp, to solve that doubt was able,
Since Julian and July'un were stripped of mark and label?

How those two youths were overhauled by doctors and by nurses,
How cruel Fate, by kingly lips, was overwhelmed with curses,
And how at last, they spun a brown to solve the dreadful myst'ry,
My loyalty's been so outraged, I leave it all to hist'ry.

The test applied turned out all wrong, and at the coronation,
The peasant's son, and not the prince, was crowned to rule the nation;
And from that hour, straight down to this, each wielder of the sceptre
Has had no more of regal blood than Cromwell, the Protector!

And yet, despite of the mishap, the old land's fairly thriving,
The workers make the wheels spin round, no matter who is driving.
The blue blood in the veins of kings, take this, my friends, as sartin,
And right divine are, if not wrong, my eye and Betty Martin!

ST. CRISPIN.

I'm not a saint; I sometimes wish I were,
   And then I laugh at such a strange conceit;
Clean shaved, and dressed with sacerdotal care,
   With stockings red and sandals for my feet.
Stay! that's not right, I firmly do attest
The saints of old were not so finely dressed.

I never saw a saint in all my life,
   But I have read they were not over clean,
That some were peaceful, others fond of strife,
   That few were fat, and many were quite lean;
That some wore bucklers, and were armed like knights,
While others led the lives of anchorites.

I've read how Dunstan tweaked the devil's nose,
   How Bridget thought her beauty quite a sin;
Another spent her life in making clothes
   For friendless mortals who were short of tin.
How Patrick banished all the snakes and toads,
And how they built their shrines by four cross roads.

I've read of one, St. Dennis, by the bye,
   Of France, I think; of that I'm not quite sure,
Of whom, 'tis said, but p'r'aps 'tis all a lie
   He walked, without his head, seven miles or more.
Still, there's no telling, saints have done strange things,
And some have flown, without a sign of wings!

I've read too of Saint Brandon, foolish man,
   A saintly tar—at least he once set sail,
To make a convert of a noted khan,
   And landed on the broad back of a whale.
Still, he was saved! a miracle! no doubt,
He got inside, like Jonah—then got out.

And then there's one, whose name I quite forget,
   That put to sea with three boys in a tub,
Who on the highway were by robbers met,
   Who lived on natives when they wanted grub.
And while o'er saintly deeds I used to revel,
I found that one, at cheating, beat the devil!

I've read a deal of saints, but I forget
   All, save such as he of Erin's Isle,
Whom Satn tempted to his wide-spread net
   With that sweet morsel, yclept a woman's smile.
I've read of—where's the book? just let let me see,
That precious saint of saints of Hungary.

I read a deal of them in former days,
   But where's the mind that can remember all?
I dream of one, above, beyond all praise,
   The good Saint Crispin of the cobbler's stall;
He was a saint, a Christian saint, I'm sure,
Who spent his life in lifting up the poor.

I'll sing of Crispin, brightest, purest, best,
   The saint, whose day each craftsman loves to keep;
And this, I swear, if ever I confessed
   The host of sins o'er which I daily weep,
No other saint or priest could ever move
Me to confession, but the one I love.

They tell us he was born in ancient Rome,
   Beside old Tiber's pestilential flood,
That idly rolls beneath St. Peter's dome,
   Round which, of late, has gathered so much mud—
A prince despoiled by jealousy or malice,
And driven out, like young Jones, from a palace.

We are not told the quarrel that prevailed
   Between the Crispin family and Tiberius,

(The greatest crime on earth is having failed)
   Whate'er it was, it ended somewhat serious.
Now note the error, or no blame to us—
For that Tiberius, just read Maximus!

"Thank Heaven," cried Crispin, they have not o'er ta'en us!"
   The night was dark, the campaign country damp,
Then with his younger brother, Crispianus
   He started off to Soissons on the tramp.
In this respect, we've followed Crispin well—
For where we have not tramped, no man can tell.

From town to town, Saint Crispin's sons have raced,
   Their clams and stirrup oft their only load;
No few by pickets, for deserting, chased,
   No sooner off the seat than on the road,
Through storm or sunshine, blinding hail or snow,
In search of work, or pleasure, off they'd go.

Through slush and mud, o'er many a swampy bog,
   Their only light the glowworm in the grass;
The only sound, the croaking of a frog,
   The screech of bat, or braying of an ass
Turned out to rest its bones, or stay its hunger,
By lazzaroni, anglais costermonger.

Long ere the dawning of the coming day
   Had flooded earth with beauty and with light,
All sense of fear had fairly given way—
   Sunk far behind, and left them to their flight—
While seeds of Hope that trembling Faith had nourished,
Took firmer root, and, thus befriended, flourished.

At length, the morning broke, and singing birds
   Sent forth from every bush their hymn of praise,
And then awoke the drowsy flocks and herds
   To romp or play, or steadily, to graze;
And by each barn and byre, from swelling throat,
Each strutting cock sent forth his clarion note.

For many a week, they wandered on and on,
   No trav'lling ticket brought them food or bed;
Like him they followed, God's immortal son,
   They lacked a spot whereon to rest their head.
A bag of meal was all their stock and store;
Like true disciples—they were very poor.

In village after village, Crispin preached;
   What would we give to read his sermons now?
At length, the borderland of France was reached,
   The sunny south, where laden vine-trees bow,
Where bottles filled with sparkling champaign crack,
And modern priests give new wines to the rack!

How many times the world has swung around?
   What mighty changes have come o'er each scene,
Since Crispin first set foot on that strange ground,
   Where froggy's thought a dainty for a queen?
Mont Cenis then was void of rail and tunnel,
And snow-clad Alps possessed no human funnel.

Outspent and weary, poor and destitute,
   But full of faith, and trusting in his God,
The brave Old Saint, true courage, absolute,
   Saw naught in danger, but heaven's chastening rod:
He did not sigh regretfully for home,
And, like our churchmen, hanker after Rome.

However Crispin learned to make a shoe,
  We're not informed by any of the sages;
I've searched and vainly searched, ay, through and through,
  The whole of Gibbon's grand historic pages;
I've pondered o'er each ancient tomb and missal,
But nothing tells me how he learned to bristle.

Beneath the gathered dust of by-gone years;
  The truth lies buried far from mortal sight;
And I, at least, have got my doubts and fears.
  That naught that man can do will bring to light,
The crans, tuition, or the efforts made,
Whereby these brothers learnt the gentle trade.

An old tradition clothed in curious rhyme,
  About two Princes in the Weald of Kent
Has floated to us on the stream of time:
  It tells us how their cash was fairly spent,
How, leaving home, they wandered up and down
T'escape the shadow of their parents' frown.

It tells how Crispin and his brother won,
  With boots and shoes, admittance into court,
And how each brother proved to be the son
  Of some great king who'd drifted far a-port!
How fair Ursula loved the elder brother—
And naught could ever turn her to another.

But, in my history, you shall nothing find,
  No vile anacronism like this foolish tale,
That leaves a shadow of a doubt behind,
  That makes you say, "It's very like a whale."
You shall not, when my history's fairly told,
With old Polonius, cry out, "I am sold."

They learned the trade, and that's enough for me,
  They wrought in Soissons for a year or more;
They never crossed the channel or the sea,
  They freely gave to Soissons' starving poor.
They prayed and preached, and converts quickly made,
And earned a living at the good old trade.

They died as martyrs die, whose burning faith,
  Is more than antidote to every wrong;
They had no fear of prison or of death,
  No cry of suffering ever left their tongue;
The block to them was but a stepping stone,
And all they did, proclaimed "God's will be done."

THE FRENCH BOOTMAKERS' CHALLENGE AND THE REPLY.

In answer to an article that appeared in the MONITEUR DE LA CORDONNERIE written to depreciate the great renown of English bootmakers, I, as proprietor and editor of ST. CRISPIN, inserted a challenge to find a given number of Englishmen to work an equal number of French craftsmen for the sum of £100. The editor of the French Leather Trade Journal replied in a poem of which the following is a poor translation by your humble servant. In my reply thereto, I thought fit to follow the example set. The result will be found to follow the effort of M. Vincent, a French poet of no slight reputation among the humble class of his countrymen. This peaceful challenge ended in smoke.—J. B. L.

Men of Paris, Lyons, Bordeaux,
  Men of Marseilles and of Lisle,
Up and buckle on your armour,
  And at Victory's altar kneel;
English workmen give you challenge,
  Not to pillage, burn or slay,
But to prove that you are better
  Skilled in leather craft than they.

France has always borne the sceptre,
  O'er the realms where fancy rules,
And the world has been contented
  With the teachings of her schools;

We have married Roman richness
　　To the matchless grace of Greece,
And given to their triumphs
　　A new and longer lease.

Ancient nobles, brave patricians,
　　Clothed their feet in shoes of gold,
Covered them with costly jewels,
　　Torn from nations weak and old.
We have jewels, richer, rarer,
　　Torn from no one but ourselves,
Borrowed from the realms of Fancy,
　　Cut and set by Crispin elves.

We have shorn barbaric splendour,
　　Freed the gold from cumbering ore,
Given each a purer aspect
　　Than it held in days of yore;
We have swept away the rubbish
　　That has clung to ancient laws,
And have placed in truer "settings"
　　All that won the world's applause.

Shall we then give way to neighbours,
　　And confess our courage fails?
Shall we miss the wind that's blowing,
　　Sent by Chance to fill our sails?
Men of Paris, Men of Bordeaux,
　　Grasp the awl by way of lance,
Men of Marseilles, Lisle and Lyons,
　　Strike for Glory and for France.

THE REPLY.

Rouse the courage of your people,
　　Stir them up to bloodless strife,
We reserve our strength and valour
　　For the peaceful arts of life!
We are sick of war and carnage,
　　Tales of blood, and hate, and wrong,
Sick of seeing right down-trodden,
　　And the triumph of the strong!

We have sent the flaming cross round,
　　Far athwart the Scottish hills,
We have roused our Celtic brothers,
　　Heroes of a thousand "mills!"
We have stirred the depths of Welshland,
　　Roused the Manxmen from their sleep;
Sounded all the lowest levels,
　　Reached the heights where eagles sweep:

Stitchmen, pegmen, nail and screwmen,
　　All are eager for the fight,
And the watchword they have chosen,
　　Is "May God defend the Right!"
Rivetters with iron idols,
　　Longingly await the day,
And the artful, tricky clobberer,
　　With his idol built of clay.

They've not stolen from the ancients,
　　Strut not they in borrowed plumes;
Still, they profit by experience,
　　And have faith that victory looms.
They have not secured the harvests
　　That the brave of old had sown;
They have taste, and skill, and labour,
　　They dare bravely call their own.

Shades of Hamilton and Edwards,
　　Shades of Morton and McGrath,
Rouse ye from your lengthened slumbers,
　　And assist us in the war;
Shades of Rees, and Mew, and Bradshaw,
　　Rouse ye from the rotting mould,
Teach our men to win such honours,
　　As your confreres won of old.

Shades of Reynolds and McIvor,
　　Shades of Devlin and the rest,
Up! and teach our Cortis, Players,
　　To do their brilliant best.
Up! Macfarlane! up! ap Griffith!
　　Up! ye brave "dons," one and all!
Show the Frenchmen how ye wrestle—
　　How ye rush at Honour's call!

Tell to Lyons, Paris, Bordeaux,
　　And to Lisle-men, good and true,
We are eager for the onset
　　To this peaceful Waterloo;
To this trial in skill and craftship
　　That St. Crispin taught of yore,
Ere he died for truth at Soissons,
　　To live for evermore!

NOTE.—The proper names mentioned in the foregoing poem are those of celebrated makers and closers of the past and present. Certain technical terms have been employed, but it will be sufficient to note that a "clobberer" is a patcher up of old shoes, who employs clay in the place of leather in bottoming, and that "don" is the common word used by shoemakers for men of superior ability at their craft.

THE BALLET GIRL.

I was only a child, and I wondering stared
  at the mutes that stood at our door,
When we lived in the terrace at Islington,
  and kept the whole first floor;
And I wondered, too, at the great black
  coach that drove up a moment after,
And know that I greeted its long-tailed
  steeds with welcoming shouts and
  laughter.

I was only a child, and I nothing knew of
  the loss I had suffered then,
How lips that had kissed me were closed
  for aye, and never would kiss me again;
How, just like a vessel, with anchor adrift,
  I was floated upon the world;
I was only a child with pretty blue eyes,
  And locks that my mother had curled.

I knew that my father had stayed at home,
  and my mother had watched by his side,
Though stowed away in a neighbour's
  room, on the night my father died;
I remember how mother, dressed all in
  black, with tears running down her face,
Passed through the door, and stepped into
  a coach that moved at a snail-like pace.

I remember the man in a sable dress who
  rode on the board behind,
And the neighbours had each put a shutter
  up, or drawn down a parlour blind;
And the nodding plumes on the horses'
  heads, and the words of the pitying
  crowd;
But I'd only seen father asleep in bed, and
  not in his milk white shroud.

I had seen a box with handles bright on the
  shoulders of men high borne,
With a big black plate screwed on to the
  lid they had fastened that very morn;
But I never knew, and I never dreamt,
  when they bore him slowly away,
That I'd seen the last of my poor old dad
  on the morn of that yesterday.

I was only a child when my mother strove
  to win us our daily bread,
And, hour by hour, would sit and stitch,
  with aching heart and head,
And only a child when her eyes went
  blind, and she could no longer sew,
And she sat and wrung her hands in grief
  with nought in the world to do.

It was then, I remember, a showman came,
  and gently knocked at the door,
And mother ran down, and invited him to
  our room on the garret floor,
And they talked of father who had passed
  away, and debated what could be done,
And so it was I was taught to dance, and
  my work on the stage begun.

In a neighbouring street, near the Lower
  Road, dwelt a man who had danced at
  "The Lane,"
Whose limbs had grown stiff with age and
  gout, and who never would dance again;
And in less than a month he had tutored
  me to move with the ease of a sprite,
When I was engaged as an extra girl for
  the "Lane" on a Boxing Night.

I was only a child in the ways of the
  world, and I'd never seen a stage,
And how happy I was as I tripped it home
  with my first-earned weekly wage,
And happier still when I asked her to feel
  the pound that she could not see,
And saw the bright smile of the dear blind
  soul who had laboured so hard for me.

The pantomime ran till the Easter term,
  and the money kept rolling in—
It was more than enough for our meagre
  wants, but less than the wage of sin,
And, no matter how long, or how hard I
  wrought, I was always ready to go,
And evermore gay when I heard them say
  "There's a call for an extra show."

So, for many a year till my mother died,
  we managed to jog along,
And, despite of the traps that bestrew the
  stage, I never sank into wrong,
But I soon found out that the brazen slut
  gets ever the bigger wage,
And that merit alone is seldom found in
  front of the modern stage.

I have practised hard for the foremost rank,
  but my struggles are all in vain,

A lord, or a duke, or a millionaire, and not dancing will win at "The Lane,"
So, I'm still at the back, where I was at the start, and there I am like to be,
Yet I envy not those, in their costly clothes, who skip in the front of me.

When my work is done, and I change my dress, there's no carriage to wait at the door,
I am only a simple ballet girl, and that's why I don't earn more;
I've no sealskin jacket, no wristlet of gold, nor diamond blazing with light;
They are not to be bought with a ballet girl's pay, of at most a crown a night.

I am not the pet of the manager, I am useful, and that is all,
And I do not sit when my dancing's done bejewelled in box or stall;
But I thank my stars, and lay me down, when my nightly toil is o'er;
I have nothing done to sully the name of those who have gone before.

—o—

THE VILLAGE DORCAS.

I says as how she be a lady,
  (I don't care what other folk say),
Her looks arn't got nothen' to do wi' it—
  I don't say they be over gay.
She didn't make her face nor her figger,
  She didn't have the pickin' o' them;
And if they beant handsome or pretty,
  Let Nature herself bear the blame.

Her cheeks, they ain't painted like roses,
  Her figger ain't faultless, I own;
But prettiness, lad, why, lor love yer!
  It fades away arter it's blown.
She arn't larnt to play the pianny.
  She hasn't had time d'yer see,
So I listen to all she be sayin'
  And that be the music for me.

You arn't heerd her soft words o' comfort,
  You arn't seen her sit by your side,
When your fine-weather friends ha' forsook yer,
  And the white horse was harnessed to ride,
You arn't had a child in its cradle,
  You arn't had a sick, ailing wife,
Whose faces were burnt up with fever,
  Whose lives were a part of your life.

You ain't seen her, fearless o' danger,
  Go forth in the darkness of night,
To watch by the sick and weak hearted,
  And bear half the brunt of the fight;
Or you wouldn't say she wasn't a lady,
  You wouldn't call her ugly or plain,
But 'ud say, as I does, she's a hangel—
  A hangel without any stain.

You ask what she's good for—I'll tell ye:
  She's sound to the innermost core,
She ain't 'fraid o' catching the fever,
  She ain't above helping the poor
I have seen her walk into a cottage
  Where darkness filled every room,
And the pure light that shot from her features
  Dispelled every atom of gloom.

Now don't say she isn't a lady
  If we're to be brothers and friends,
For it causes my warm blood to tingle
  Right down to my tall finger ends.
You may curse every rogue in creation,
  (And that reaches out pretty far),
But you don't speak a word if I knows it,
  That means any wrong against her.

You may talk about preachers and churches,
  But what have they done, lad, for me?
You may talk about books filled with sarments,
  As larnèd as ever could be;
But I tell ye I don't understand 'em,
  I want summat plainer to read,
A helpin' hand stretched to the suff'rer,
  A gospel put into a deed.

Religion arn't talking or praying
  It bean't in a speech or a song;
It isn't in crying out goodness,
  It arn't often seen in a throng;
Religion be kindness an' mercy,
  As much o' them ere as yer please;
And as for this lady, lor bless yer—
  Why, isn't she built up of these?

—o—

POEMS FOR CHILDREN.

I.—THE AGE OF THE WORLD.

How strange are the questions you ask, child—
  The age of the world is unknown;
That secret is Nature's, not man's, child,
  Yes, Nature's, and Nature's alone.
We guess, but there's naught comes of guessing,
  We search, but no answer is won;
The volumes of stone at our feet, child,
  Lie hid from the light of the sun.

That secret can never be ours, child,
  'Tis hidden too deeply away;
Its records lie buried beneath us,
  Deep under the marl and the clay;
Deep under the vitrified rocks, child,
  Deep under the wide rolling waves,
Crowding the beach with their refuse,
  And hiding their treasures in caves.

Wise men who have thought through the ages,
  Undaunted by dangers around,
Fierce eyes that pierced through the darkness,
  That deepens where truth may be found;
Confess they have searched, and searched vainly,
  To gather the answer you crave;
The age of the world has been lost child,
  The past, the dead past, is its grave.

—o—

II.—SHAKSPEARE.

Why does Shakspeare live to day, mother,
  Who died so long ago?
Can a mortal be immortal,
  In this world of wail and woe?
Tell me how he left the grave, mother,
  And evermore doth stay?
Tell me why, while thousands perish,
  He lives for us to day?

Do you see yon pale-faced star, my child,
  In the dark sky overhead?
It has shone through countless ages,
  And the universe has led.
It has lighted all the world, child,
  It has triumphed o'er the night,
It has lit earth's darkest corners,
  With its everlasting light.

'Tis the Shakspeare of the heavens, my child,
  The leader of its race;
It was never meant to die, my child,
  And leave no living trace.
It has lived, and led, and leadeth still,
  And onward still must go,
Till the universe shall perish
  In its final overthrow.

Why does Shakspeare ride to day, mother,
  In that triumphant car?
Does he ride the world of darkness,
  And shine out like a star?
Does he lead the host of mortals,
  By burning love and light?
Does he drive away the darkness,
  And triumph o'er the night?

It is even so, the mother said,
  You have guessed the truth, my child,
By the genius of his life he lives,
  By his greatness Death is foiled:
By the light he scatters o'er the land,
  By his powers to lead and save,
And the magic of his wondrous gifts,
  He has triumphed o'er the grave.

—o—

JOY AND SORROW.

A dainty little maiden,
With care and sorrow laden,
  Her burthen told to me;
And pitying her sorrow,
I promised ere to-morrow,
  To set the maiden free.

Ere day was fairly over,
I met the maiden's lover,
  And beckoned him to me.
And ere the daylight vanished,
All care and sorrow banished
  The weeping maid was free.

Oh! happy, happy maiden,
No longer sorrow laden,
  But joyous, gay and free.

So happy with thy lover,
All care and sorrow over,
  A queen might envy thee.

What means that bell a-tolling,
That muffled sound now rolling
  O'er grassy knoll and lea?
Who is the favoured mortal,
Now entering death's portal,
  From sin and sorrow free?

What maiden is that weeping,
What manly form there sleeping?
  Come, prithee, tell to me;
Is she that dainty maiden,
Once more with sorrow laden,
  No longer gay and free?

Alas! the dream is over,
It is the maiden's lover
  Whose coffin now I see;
For him she long will languish,
Her life all care and anguish,
  No more will she be free.

—o—

SPRING AND SUMMER.

Climbing the hill of life,
  With light and springy tread,
What pleasant sights we see,
Joy, void of care and strife,
  Sunshine through clouds o'erhead,
Blossoms on bush and tree.

Green lanes with hedgerows fair,
  Footpaths through meadows green,
Sunned banks with flowers spread,
Larks singing overhead,
  Green woods with paths between,
Pleasure bereft of care.

Streams singing songs of joy,
  Boughs rocking leaves to rest,
Lambs skipping by our side—
Beauties that never cloy—
  Birds chirping round their nest,
Joy riding with the tide.

Bees culling sweets from flowers,
  Girls snatching nosegays sweet,
Cows browsing in the shade,
Freshness in spur and blade,
  Green grass beneath our feet,
Love in a thousand bowers.

Life is a merry round,
  Life is a holiday,
Life is a scene of bliss,
The wide world enchanted ground,
  Where fairies skip and play,
One lasting lover's kiss.

Dreams, dreams, how quickly sped!
  Cold blasts are hurrying by,
Dead flowers strew our path,
Clouds thunder forth their wrath,
  Streamlets now moan and sigh,
And graves now claim their dead.

—o—

AUTUMN AND WINTER.

The snow is falling fast,
  I'm getting old and weak,
My limbs grow stiff and cold;
My comfort's in the past,
  And deep cut in my cheek,
Are tracks where tears have rolled.

The sense of memory's gone,
  Mine eyes are growing dim,
And sounds make no impress;
This lessens and grows less,
  And these with vapour swim,
And these have left me lone.

Those who shared my youth,
  Have left me none to share,
And what they had they've lost;
He who pledged me truth,
  He who won to wear,
Is changed into a ghost.

Give me room to pass,
  Unloose the river's dam;
What is death to me?
A confluence with the sea,
  Return to what I was,
The loss of what I am.

Old world, old world, good night!
  The darkness gathers round,
And folds me all within,

Where there is no light,
　Where echo hears no sound,
Where souls have ceased to sin.

Thus, thus, we come and go,
　Climbing life's sunny steep,
A resting place to find ;
Leaving no trace behind,
　Saving the tears we weep,
And crosses of our woe.

—o—

THE SEA NYMPH'S HOME.

Empty and void, 'twas once a home
　Where strife ne'er entered,
With pearl-enamelled corridor
And walls and dome
　Where joy was centred.
'Twas here a sea nymph loved and sang,
　Both late and early,
And charmèd echoes hid behind
　Those walls so pearly.

Empty and void, without a trace
　Of life within it,
But whence those sounds so full of grace—
　So infinite ?
They're echoes of the sea nymph's song
　Ere she departed,
The living echoes still prolong
　The strain she started.

'Twill never cease while echoes live ;
　But still prevailing
O'er time, shall ever breathe to give
　Comfort unfailing.
The children playing on the sand,
　In wonder listen,
Their little souls, thus moved, expand—
　Their bright eyes glisten.

Sing on, sweet echo, in thy pearly home,
　Thy natal chamber,
Thou art secure, within thy living tomb,
　As fly in amber,
The listening ear is never robbed by thee,
　Never cheated,
The self-same song of soft, sweet minstrelsy,
　Is aye repeated.

—o—

A SIMILE.

I heard a leaflet whisp'ring
　While standing 'neath the trees,
" I am never tired of dancing
　To the music of the breeze ;
　　Like a racer I am prancing,
　　Like a giddy girl I'm dancing."

The summer sun is shining,
　And standing 'neath the trees,
I listen for a whisper
　From the leaflet in the breeze.
　　But, alas ! no more it mutters,—
　　Short and fitfully it flutters.

The autumn leaves are falling,
　And lying in the slough
Is the leaflet I saw dancing
　In the springtide on the bough ?
　　From the time the rude blast kissed her
　　She was never heard to whisper.

—o—

ART.

Life's grosser thoughts were never made for Art,
　She claims alone the thoughts that are most pure,
Those only that at heaven's prompting start
　And find their haven on the heavenly shore.

I would that I could live for Art alone,
　And by such living keep my soul aye free.
Could count my tributes by my art-work done,
　And all my gains in what she gave to me.

I'd paint and sing from early dawn till eve,
　Turn ears and eyes to paths of excellence,
Give all to her for whom I pray to live,
　And swell the total of her affluence.

—o—

THE SICK CLOWN AND THE LOST LETTER.

In a damp fœtid cell, near the square called Soho,
Dwelt an old circus clown who had been with Ducrow;
The merriest mime that the world ever knew,
Once prized for the sake of the crowds that he drew.
He'd a son christened Jemmy, a promising lad,
But the gossips reported he'd gone to the bad;
And a daughter for beauty;—well, not in the race,
If beauty is nowhere except in the face.
    But then you're aware
    The true " William " pear
    Was never good looking:
It's not always the fruit that wears the best suit,
    In eating or cooking,
    That turns out the best.
    Put such things together
    And ask yourself whether
    Face beauty's a test.
It was down in that cellar so cold and so damp
    Tom Bannercroft lay,
No light but the rays of a flickering lamp
    One cold winter day.
  Racked and writhing with pain
  That effected his brain,
And stirred-up past scenes in the circus again.
Then he muttered, " My gal, I'm so faint and so weak!
Wipe the cold, sweaty dew off my brow and my cheek!
Then you've not seen the postman, you've not heard his knock?"
" No father, no letter, and past nine o'clock!"
" I suppose its all true what they say of my lad?"
" No father, they lie; he's not gone to the bad!"
" Then, where is his pity for me and for you,
If all that they say of my Jemmy's untrue?"
But checked by her words, as he fell back in pain,
He muttered "You're right Bess come kiss me again,
I wander a bit and my thoughts are untrue,
There is no more of badness, in Jemmy than you,
But why don't he write, 'tis a month now and more,
Since Jemmy's last letter was left at the door."
Mistakes about letters are not over rare,
I once was commissioned to carry a pair;
    But I mixed them somehow,
    And knowing no better,
    Gave Brown Jone's letter,
    Which led to a row.
In the year seventy-four when the well in Lloyd's square,
Once famed for its waters so bright and so clear,
    Was closed—the pump lost its spout
    And its handle,
    Both stolen—no doubt.
With a deal of reflection, at this time 'twas planned
By the big-wigs who governed St. Martin's-le-Grand,
    To create pillar-boxes,—
    As post-office proxies,—
Where letters that persons are pleased to indite
May be dropped, like chance kids, in the dead of the night,
In that damp fœtid cell, near the square called Soho,
Where stretched on his bed lay the clown of Ducrow,
    Poor Betsy was crying;
    Her father seemed dying.
But ere the act closes, and time is no more,
A lad upon crutches walked in at the door,
" How's father?" he cried, with a voice full of fear,
The clown gave a start and then beckoned him near:
His dull eyes grew brighter,—" I'm bad, very bad!
Come tell your poor father what's happened my lad!
And why didn't you write —have you been out of town?"
" I wrote, but just stay while I summons Jack Brown!
Let my pal tell the tale, for he knows it far better,
Here, Jack, let them know what you did with my letter!"
" Well I'll tell you," says Jack, " when Jim broke his thighs,
And was took to the accident ward down at Guy's
When the stays and the net and the rope broke away,
And he fell on the seats from the flying trapeze;
His last words to me, at I bade him good night,
Were ' Look in that pocket, that 'ere on the right:
There's a letter with money, just to help the old man;
Drop it into a pillar as quick as you can!"
Well the first one I comes to was that in Lloyd's square
And all that I knows is, I dropped it in there."
" Yes that seems all right, you couldn't have done better,"
Said Betsy, " but what has become of the letter?"
" I dunno," said Jack. " Then I fancy I do—
Was there ever on earch such a blockhead as you?
You've mistaken the pump for a pillar, my lad;
And that's why the letter has failed to reach dad.
The whole thing's explained—there's no longer a doubt,
Jim's letter went in where the handle came out.
" Don't mind it," cried Jemmy " it's all over now,
I've a purse full of gold," and a smile crossed his brow:
" They have made a collection to put me all right,
Since that terrible fall on that terrible night;
And as for the loss, 'tis a mere bagatelle,
It was meant for the sick and has gone to the well.'
But, as for you, Bet, you are clever, no doubt,
You've bin busily shoving your clothes up the spout!"
To my tragical story you'll deem this all folly,
But the sick man recovered, then why not be jolly;
And his boy, little Jim, has remained to this day,
The wonder of wonders upon the trapeze·
    And as for Jack Brown,
    He has lately turned clown,
    Got married to Betsy;
And they live altogether away from Soho,
In a neat little villa at Stratford-by-Bow
The pair, little Jim, and the clown of Ducrow.

ALDERMAN STUBBS,
Cheesemonger and Numismatist.

In a cheesemonger's shop, just as broad as 'tis wide,
In a narrow-guaged street that runs from Cheap-
side,
    Traded Alderman Stubbs,
And there ranged on shelves were ripe Stiltons ga-
lore,
And Gloucester, and Cheddar strewed over the floor,
    And butter in tubs.
In the year '56 he started, unaided,
And, up to the present time, quietly traded
    In that narrow street;
And there too he dwelt, in the kitchen below,
But having grown rich he determined to go
    To some pleasant retreat—
That is, after business was done for the day,
And the folks in the City had all gone away.
The spot he selected was Stratford by Bow—
It is easy to reach by the rail as you know,
Or by tramcar and 'bus, but the latter are slow.
The villa he rented was semi-detached,
And its garden for neatness, I'm told can't be
matched,
With a neat wicket gate that, for safety, is latched.
    There he rested in clover,
    When business was over,
    But there isn't a joy
    In the world that don't cloy.
When a man lives by dealing in butter and cheese
And moves from the City for comfort and ease,
A change in his habits will come by degrees.
At first o'er his day-book and ledger he'd ponder
Then count up his takings each evening and won-
der
    How business had grown;
But day book and ledger were heavy to bear,
And one night he lost them before he got there
    On his journey from town.
    So he gave up the plan,
    Like a sensible man,
And said, "From my mind every thought about
butters—
Shall cease as I screw up the bar to the shutters!"
Now Alderman Stubbs had a neighbour and friend,
Who, whenever he had any spare cash to spend,
Would sink it in *China* without hesitation,
In Chelsea and Worcester, but not in the *nation*,
    He bought basins and jugs,
    Plates, dishes and mugs,
    And whatever his store,
    Still kept thirsting for more,
Till you would have thought he'd enough and to
spare,
To start as a dealer in crockery ware.
Mr. Stubbs had long envied the taste he displayed,
And the marvellous bargains his neighbour had
made,
And thought that a hobby might supplement trade.
    Then "What shall I start?
    I've no knowledge of art;
    Ah! I've hit on the thing,
    That money will bring.
I'll turn numismatist—read Ruding and Clark
And Fountaine, and all the great authors of mark,
I'll do it," he said, and in less than a week,
He was posted in coins that are scarce and antique,
And tokens that connoisseurs prize as unique.
It mattered not what in the shop might be sold,
He inspected the copper, the silver and gold,
And the string of each five-shilling packet was
broken
In fear that he might miss a rare coin or token;
And, night after night, as he sat in his chair,
He'd empty his pockets of coins old and rare,
    Of all sorts and sizes,
    (Yet not many prizes,)
But, of course, all collections must have a begin-
ning,
If you don't make a start, you'll have no chance of
winning.
Then he courted acquaintance with navvies, all
round,
And others who toil, like the mole, underground,
And bribed them to show him the coins they had
found.
It was once Stubb's plan, ere he took down the
shutters,
To read the quotations of cheese and of butters;
But now, all was changed, he skipped the quota-
tions
Of prices that ruled in all markets and nations,
To read every author from Eckhel to Carter
Who fill up their pages about Numismarta.
One night as he sat in his favourite chair,
He got down his books and began to compare,
His coins with the plates with great niceness and
care;
When suddenly starting, he sprang to his feet,
With such force, I am told, that he upset his seat.
"What's this?" he exclaimed, " by heavens! here's a
prize!"
And he stared at a coin, with his large goggle eyes,
"Here's a beautiful angel!" "A what?" cried his
spouse,
(From such simple words have been bred many
rows;)
" An Angel" cried Stubbs, "an angel, my dear,"
"Then, I'll soon start her off, I'll have no angels
here!"
    But of course, when Stubbs told her
    To come and behold her,
    She saw that his angel was old
    And not formed of flesh, but of gold.
In fact, 'twas a coin, as you very well know,
That was cast like a chequer—not struck at a
blow!
With a dragon a saint was determined to slay
With a very long spear, in a very queer way;
And the coin bore the face of the first angel made,
And the date when the angels first started in
trade!

"To-morrow," said Stubbs to his wife, "take my word,
To the British Museum, I'm off, like a bird!
At the first leisure moment, I'm off like a shot,
To see if this angel has fallen or not!
And he went like a bird, as you see, if you'll try,
When I tell you he quitted the shop in a fly!
    His star was ascendant,
    He saw the attendant,
    And told him his mission,
    And void of suspicion,
    He ushered him in,
    And there in a case,
    Staring right in his face,
    Was the angel of sin!
The angel of commerce, excuse me this time,
I called commerce sin, for the want of a rhyme.
He took out the coin, and before he could speak,
The man in attendance cried out "Its unique;"
"My eye!" thought the butterman, "then I've a squeak!"
The coins gathered up, one by one, and put back,
Save the angel that playfully dropped down a crack.
"Hallo!" cried the keeper of coins, "here, just stay!
What you've stolen the angel! come back, thief, I say,
And what's more than suspicious, you're running away!"
"I've taken no coin," "Mr. Stubbs loudly hollered!
But the end of it was, the cheesemonger was collered.
    Then searching began,
    And the poor Alderman
    Turned white as a ghost,
    And when, old and yellow,
    They found the coin's fellow,
    He sang, "All is lost!"
'My God! said the Alderman—" this is a strange ill?
He was not the first man who'd been floored by an angel,
I am charged as a robber," then with tears running over,
'This ends all my thoughts about living in clover
The envy I felt towards Jones was my ruin,
The charms of that angel completes my undoing!"
Thus he cried, in despair, as he paced his dark cell,
With a feeling of dread, that no mortal can tell.
    But through a small chink,
    Of that horrible sink
      Of iniquity,
    Fell a small spec of light,
    To illumine the night,
      In crooked obliquity.
Then footsteps were heard, coming nearer and nearer,
And whispering voices, first faint and then clearer,
    And then, mid the prattle,
    He heard the key's rattle,
And now as the turnkey throws open the floor,
The Alderman stands in the daylight once more.
    The angel was found,
    And the Butterman, free,
    Got home safe and sound
    In time for his tea,
    Where this innocent martyr
    Cried, "Damn Numismata!"
And now, every night, when he puts up his shutters,
Mr. Stubbs sleeps to dream about nothing but butters,
Or if he by chance smokes a pipe at his ease,
The mightiest matter he thinks of—is cheese.

GIVE ME THE STREAM.

I've climbed old Scotia's heathery hills,
    And roamed her mountain-guarded dales;
But there's no spot on earth I love
    Like Swakeley's deep and wooded vales.
I've sat by many a mountain burn,
    And loved to hear it fret and roar;
But still the stream of streams for me,
    Runs not on Scotland's rugged shore.
    Give me the stream, the sacred stream,
      Whose banks I trod with Annie,
    That sings beneath those tall pine boughs
      That lent their shade to Annie.

When 'neath their silent shades I sit,
    And list the stream's soft lullaby,
I think I hear her gentle voice,
    And see her fair form flitting by.
But I may sit the live-long day
    And vainly count the heather's charms;
For where, oh, where's the burnie's song
    That brings my Annie to these arms?
    Give me the stream, the sacred stream,
      Whose banks I trod with Annie,
    That sings beneath those tall pine boughs
      That lent their shade to Annie.

I've trod Gleniffer's sunny braes,
    And careless climbed the banks of Ayr;
But Swakeley's vales have charms for me,
    No other spot on earth can share.
There let me lie amid the fern
    That decks the streamlet's rising shore,
And cull from Memory's crowded page,
    The joys that thrilled my soul of yore.
    Give me the stream, the sacred stream,
      Whose banks I trod with Annie,
    That sings beneath those tall pine boughs
      That lent their shade to Annie.

A FRAGMENT.

The breath I breathe is surely not my own,
The thought that moves me, was by others sown;
The passions, too, by which my soul is stirred,
Have oft, in others, praise and blame incurred;
I move, I live, I dream that I am free,
That earth and heaven were formed to succour me.
But, what am I? a weak and fragile thing,
That nature counts not in her reckoning!
The world is moved by men who rouse and lead,
Whose every word is father to a deed;
Whose every act an effort of the mind
That cuts a path for those who trail behind.
'Tis true, I speak, I am not stricken dumb,
I go, when bidden; and, when called, I come;
But, still, the men, whom gods and angels love,
Are those whose souls have prompted them to move!

—o—

LONG AGO!

When the spell of love was broken,
    Long ago;
When its sole remaining token
    Turned to woe;
I walked this vale of sorrow,
And no comfort could I borrow
From the shadow-crowned to-morrow,
    Long ago.

My heart was sad and weary,
    Long ago;
All around was dark and dreary,
    Long ago;
Where I sipped Joy's cup—a brimmer,
And the sunshine used to glimmer—
And a pathway met the swimmer,
    All is woe.

Like a banished man I wandered,
    To and fro;
Ties of friendship rent and sundered,
    Long ago;
Icy seas of Sorrow bound me,
Not a ray of comfort found me,
Ne'er a white wing fluttered round me
    In my woe.

Every season has its blossom,
    And the snow,
Like a mantle, keeps earth's bosom
    All aglow;
Every tree, and shrub, and flower,
In woodland, field, and bower,
Forgets 'mid shine and shower,
    All its woe.

Break of day and Spring's first blossom,
    Ease my woe;
Stir the pulse that warmed my bosom
    Long ago;
Rob my brain of all its madness,
Fill my heart bowed down with sadness;
With a summer growth of gladness,
    Heal my woe.

—o—

RECOLLECTIONS OF HOME.

If I have gloried o'er a nugget found,
  Or thrilled with pride to see my wealth increase;
One simple thought my sole ambition crowned,
  'Twas here to dwell, and close my life in peace.
But like the poor who grow rich in their sleep
  And wake to find a dream was all their store,
My visioned scenes are shells cast from the deep,
  Telling of what they were, and nothing more.

The farm neglected, fences broke away;
   The homestead blasted by the breath of time;
Neglect and ruin jointly holding sway,
   Where once neglect was punished as a crime.
Yon water wheel as quiet as the grave,
   No more revolves beneath a miller's care;
High flags and rushes o'er its waters wave,
   And ruin, slothful ruin, everywhere.

What blighting agency has thus betrayed
   The things I love into such ruthless keep;
I see them now, and, childlike, stand dismayed,
   And turn to leave them as I turn to weep.
The scattered peasantry, whither have they fled?
   Where mighty rivers seek t' Atlantic coast,
Some try their fortune, others, long since dead;
   While all are far away, and all are lost.

—o—

SNOW FLAKES.

Fast falls the snow on a frosty night,
   On river and field, on copse and moor,
And grass, and rushes, and fields are white,
   And white the homes of the rich and poor.

Floating like feathers, dancing like flies,
   Turning and twisting on nothing but air,
Fragments of clouds from wintry skies,
   Snowflakes, snowflakes, everywhere.

Feathers from fluttering angels' wings,
   Whiter than lilies, whiter than foam,
Fresh from the fields where the summer lark sings,
   Freed from the cares of humanity's home.

Fast falls the snow on a frosty night,
   Crystals of light and children of air,
Who can follow their zig-zag flight?
   Snowflakes, snowflakes, everywhere!

—o—

HUNT THE SLIPPER.

Lads and lasses, say a score,
Form a circle on the floor.

Then, feigning customer or friend,
Inquires, "Who will a slipper mend?"

He looks around the damaged shoe,
And asks what he's required to do,
Then promises at half-past two.

Then all cry out at one set pitch,
"Hammer, hammer, stitch, stitch, stitch,
Such haste, you'd think would make him rich.

But scarce had he the work begun,
When, just to carry out the fun,
A voice exclaimed, "Is my shoe done?"

"There's some mistake," cried half a score,
"There's some mistake; enquire next door,"
Then, with a shoe, one rapped the floor.

Then, quick, the slipper's out of sight,
The customer perceives his plight,
And tries to track the slipper's flight.

He plunges here, he plunges there,
Catches a "topper" unaware,
And peals of laughter fill the air.

Anon, the hunt begins anew,
And, swift as lightning, flies the shoe,
While laughter shakes the happy crew.

Beneath their limbs, he sees it pass,
Once more he dives amid the mass,
And fixes on a tousling lass.

A tug, a tussle, and a squeal,
He's caught the slipper by the heel.

He holds it tight, the game is o'er,
The circle rises from the floor.

But many a vow and many a sigh
   Will follow as the years roll on;
A youth has caught a maiden's eye,
   An ear is pierced by a silver tone,
And youth and maiden wonder why
   Two separate hearts should beat as one.

Down quiet lanes they love to stroll,
  Through daisied meads, by running brook,
And there they read each other's soul
  As plainly as a printed book.

The slipper may have worn away,
  That game will never be forgot,
It marks a bright, red-lettered day
  That passing years will fail to blot.

The slippers on their children's feet,
  The circle seated on the floor,
When trials have made them more discreet,
  Will call to mind that game of yore.

A neighbour passing down the lane,
  Who stays to share a social chat,
Will call the dead past back again,
  And one who in the circle sat.

Her widowed love, her softened woe,
  Will burst the gates of grief once more,
And she will see, though hot tears flow,
  The merry circle on the floor.

THE RIVAL CHIEFTAINS.

On the north of the Shannon, ruled Patrick O'Brien,
A brave Irish chieftain, but given to lyin';
He had hair black as coal, and eyes like two stars,
And his life was made up of contentions and wars.
When he wasn't engaged in the thick of the battle,
He was courting a wench, or lifting of cattle.

On the south of the Shannon, dwelt Dermot M'Shane,
The dream of whose life was to slay or be slain,
And his head was a scorcher, and red as a rose,
Shone the splendid carbuncle that perched on his nose.
He was brave to a fault, in his purpose unshifting,
But too fond of the wenches, and given to lifting.

When the nights were pitch dark, M'Shane would be tryin'
To ferry the Shannon, and plunder O'Brien:
And sure history tells us in language as plain,
That O'Brien was trying to plunder M'Shane.
Them were queer sort o' days, when each man and each brother,
Thought nothing of robbing and slaying each other.

For a month at a time, Mistress Biddy O'Brien
In the home of her husband's great foe would be cryin',
But the chances of war then, inconstant as ever,
Danced first upon this, then on that side the river,
And the fact is as true, as I own it is shocking,
That, in turn, Mistress O. would be mending Mac's stocking.

"By my sowl!" mused M'Shane, on one spring afternoon,
"What a mixture of races there'll be pretty soon;
Half the carrotty polls of my long-hated foes,
Will, in turn, be as black as the blackest of crows,
And the long raven tresses that grace my fair daughters,
Will turn just as red as the Crimson Sea waters.

Then, in turn, cried M'Shane, who was proud of his race,
"There's the squint of O'Brien in my last baby's face,
And scores of young clansmen, whose hair should be red,
Have top-knots as black as the clouds overhead,
And I've noted of late, when returning from battle,
There's the sign of a cross on the back of my cattle!"

The M'Shanes and O'Briens had for centuries fought,
And plundered each other for profit and sport,
Yet, in order to keep the pure strain of each breed,
'Tween the clans, in old times, 'twas by treaty agreed,
That the women were sacred, and also that cattle
Should be killed, and not mated, straight after a battle.

But, in time, these agreements, though signed by each chief,
Like most of such contracts, in turn, came to grief,
And the clans became skewbald, and piebald and mixed,
And on both the clans' noses carbuncles had fixed!
'Twas a death-blow to pride, and the feelings it cherished,
When divisional marks, in their purity, perished.

That it's common with mortals, is well understood,
To condemn many things that are meant for their good,
And, by way of example, to prove this is true,
Take the mixture regretted by each of these two.
How it taught by reflexion the value of crosses,
And the mixture of blood both in mankind and horses.

As the clan-races blended, the longings for war
Grew weaker, and weaker, and weaker, by far;
And the blackheads and redheads, at length, settled down,
In a beautiful medium colour, called "brown,"
And the squint of O'Brien became less decided,
For the moment that treaty fell through, it divided.

If on noses, to-day, you a carbuncle trace,
It is not of a size that disfigures the face;
And I care not who hears it, M'Shane or O'Brien,
It is passed without envy, and causes no cryin';
And no Irishman living, though ever so simple,
Now questions the breed of his child by its pimple.

—o—

A LOVE STORY.

Sweet, charming Kitty Merrivale
  Came over the moorland and over the lea,
Over the mountain, and through the lone dale,
  To meet her love at the trysting tree.

Through the long pathway that threaded the corn,
  And fields of ripe clover that reddened the plane,
Under the shade of the red-berried thorn
  And nut-bearing bushes that fringed the green lane.

Onward she came with her love-lit eyes,
  Onward she came with her swift-winged feet,
Down by the stream where the kingfisher flies,
  Her own true love in the gloaming to meet.

Within the dark shade of the oak's broad crown,
  Watching and waiting her lorn lover stood,
With close-pressed lips, with a freezing frown,
  And wanting the flush of the heart's warm blood.

Nursing the heat of his pent-up wrath,
  Born of a full-mouthed gossip's tale,
With passion-lit eyes, he tracked the path
  Of charming Kitty Merrivale.

She met her love with a smile on her face,
  She left her love with her heart all torn—
She never returned to the trysting place,
  He never recalled his words of scorn.

Over the land, and over the sea,
  Ever restless by night, and restless by day,
Eager to fly from his " ain countree "
  And the maiden that stole his heart away.

Cheated and wronged, and worried and torn,
  By passions stirred by tales untrue,
Away and away, with a heart forlorn,
  The widowed lover of Kitty flew.

Where the mocking bird sings in the forest afar,
  And the wood-thrush is busily building its nest,
He, staggering, fell on the field of war,
  And, under the green turf, lies at rest.

With her desolate love hugged closely around,
  She died in the village that lies in the vale,
Nor rest, nor peace, in the world was found
  For the wandering lover that Love once crowned,
  And charming Kitty Merrivale.

—o—

LILY LOVELACE.

In a vile and dismal alley, in the purlieus of the Lane,
Grew Lily, Lily Lovelace, a flower without stain ;
How could she escape so spotless, when the flowers by her side,
Were blurred, and bruised, and blackened, by humanity's dark tide.
How could she, amidst the sqalor of the dingy, draggled crew,
Wear the features of an angel, where such sinful faces grew !

In a court so foul and loathsome, where each household reeked with crime,
Where each bud, and leaf, and blossom, was soiled with sin and slime,
Only Lily had escaped them, only she of whom I sing,
To the company of angels was a fitting offering.
Only Lily, pale-faced Lily, with her holy, azure eyes,
Bore the stamp of spotless virtue from untainted Paradise.

There were daisies trodden down by sin, and roses red with shame,
And many moths that flew around the all-consuming flame ;
There were crowds of withered snow-drops, with the leper-spots of crime ;
There were stunted, nipped-up blossoms, doomed to perish ere their prime,—
And amid them Lily Lovelace, pure and spotless as the snow,
Whom every evil influence had failed to overthrow.

There was no soul in the crowded court with Lily's to compare,
The leperous fumes of stagnant vice were present everywhere ;
She was the only trace of heaven, that I could ever see,
'Mid that seething mass of mortals, sunk in sin and misery,
The only sign of a heaven above, where sin and sorrow cease,
And the endless strife of the world is changed for everlasting peace.

There were weak and tender seedlings, that grew sicklier day by day,
With the green flies of corruption eating half their lives away ;
There were parasites that fed upon the comeliest flowers there,
On the ruddiest of the ruddy, and the fairest of the fair.
But sweet Lily, Lily Lovelace, she was fairer that the whole,
For the purity that lit her life was centred in the soul.

—o—

LOVE'S MESSAGE.

My love is standing on the bank,
  Making posies,
Beside the rushes and the sedge-growths rank,
  Gemmed with roses.
That leaf afloat upon the stream,
  Now, doubting, lingers,
That yellow leaf, discarded from the bunch,
  Has touched her fingers.

My love is standing on the river's bank,
   And there's her token—
To me a letter, to the world a blank,
   With seal unbroken.
Pass on! pass on! thine errand done,
   Thy work is over;
No more to man or womankind
   Wilt thou discover.

My love was standing on the river's bank,
   Tying posies,
This, this, to me, the leaf now sank,
   No more discloses;
There, resting on its muddy bed,
   Gone to the giver;
Laden with love no more 'twill float:
   Farewell! for ever!

A STORY FOR YULE TIDE.

The hall of Throgmorton is flooded with light,
   And a huge bunch of mistletoe dangles on high,
In a polished oak chair sits the cheery old knight,
   Whose ancestors sleep in the chancel hard by.
"Fill your cups!" he cried loudly, "and banish all sorrow!
The birthday of Christ will be with us to-morrow!"

There were youths, there were maidens, all seated around,
   There were lords, there were ladies, on every side!
And the old steeple rocked to the ripe, merry sound,
   And its bells threw their cadences over the tide—
Over the hill-tops, and over the valleys,
And through the lone wood and its long, leafless alleys.

Then the knight spoke of peace, and the gospel of love,
   And the mission of Christ for the guidance of men,
And he spoke of the cross, and the lamb, and the dove,
   And pointed their moral again and again.

It was peace, lasting peace, unstained and unbroken,
And he lifted the cross as a sign and a token.

"Now, fill up your cups, fill up to th brim.
   Here's the Army and Navy, our prid and our boast!"
He'd a son at the wars, and he ju thought of him,
   And the teaching of Christ in confusio was lost;
So, he never spoke more of the Ma crowned with Sorrow,
Of the emblem of peace, nor the coming to-morrow.

Every cup was upturned, every flago was dry,
   And the knight took his seat at th head of the board,
And never a soul in the gay companie
   Thought more of the Saviour, his mission, or word;
The tale of the God-child born 'mid the cattle,
Gave way to the charms of the turmoil of battle.

Hark! the portal bell rings, and the gates are flung back,
   And a warrior leaps from his way-weary steed,
"I have sad news to tell you, good master, alack!
   The heir of Throgmorton is classed with the dead."
The Baron turned paler than death at the story,
And nevermore sounded the trumpet of Glory.

There was weeping and wailing in Throgmorton Hall,
   And a black cloud of gloom covered all the Yule-tide;
The evergreens withered that garnished the wall,
   And the heart of the Baron was shorn of its pride.
On a far distant shore, the lost heir is sleeping,
And the lorn hearts that loved him will never cease weeping.

The tide of Old Christmas is with us once
    more,
  And we still prate of Christ in the joy
    of its bringing;
Again the rich blood of the grape we out-
    pour,
  And the moss-covered steeple is shook
    with the ringing.
But alas! and alack! we have still the
    same story
Of murder and madness, of glitter and
    glory.

—o—

SHE CAME IN THE GOLDEN SUMMER TIME.

She came in the golden summer time,
  From the emerald fields and the shady
    lane;
To the city of gold, of want, and crime.
  With never a care and never a stain.

The apple blossom was on her cheek,
  And her voice had the ring of a wild
    bird's song;
Her nest to build, and her food to seek,
  With a heart as light as the day is
    long.

From Nature's haunts, 'neath the clear
    bright sky,
  To the grimy city of ceaseless din;
From the paradise where her youth ran by,
  To the smoke that covers a world of
    sin.

She came when the sickle was hanging at
    rest,
  With the rust of sloth on its clouded
    blade,
To the city where reaper on reaper
    pressed,
  To gather the golden sheaves of trade.

The wood and the field, and the breezy
    down,
  Were all forgotten and far away;
In the bustle of life of the busy town,
  She had turned her back upon yester-
    day.
There was one little sign, and only one,
  That linked the present to days gone
    by,
That told of a love that was almost gone,
  Since she left the clear for the cloudy
    sky.

That link of the past was a faded flower,
  That struggled to live in a handful of
    mold,
And to it belonged the fairy-like power
  Of calling her back to the days of old.
Her sight never fell on that sickly thing,
  But her dim eyes shone with unwonted
    light,
And white-winged angels came whispering
  Of the happy days that had taken
    flight.

But the flower died, as all things must
    die,
  And the whispering angels were heard
    no more,
And hours and months, and years flew
    by,
  Without a thought of the days of yore.
Of the days when the flowers grew under
    her feet,
  And her heart beat time to the wild
    bird's song,
When her life was as pure as the flowers
    sweet,
  And Joy was with her the whole day
    long.

THE LAST DREAM.

In the merry, laughing, summer time,
    when all the bees were humming,
And green-backed, skipping, grasshop-
    pers, their monotone kept drumming,
I, seated on a daisied knoll, in the sha-
    dow of the wild wood,
Was spinning rhyme of the golden time—
    of the happy days of childhood.

I threaded the lane where the hawthorn
    trees hung out their red-tipt blossom,
And followed the rill to the ivy-clad mill,
    that stands in the vale's deep bosom;
I climbed the zigzag mountain path, with
    limbs that never faltered,
And could not see, for the life of me, that
    I or the world had altered.

I, musing, sat, till the gloaming came,
    and added shade to shadow,
Enfolded all the mountain tops, and
    covered moor and meadow;
Till, one by one, the stars came forth,
    and threw their radiance over
The golden grain of the burnished plain,
  And field of red-ripe clover.

"Oh! why should I dream," said I, at last, "of scenes that have passed for ever?
When every epoch of mortal life, demands some new endeavour.
When every thought of the distant past, is a grain of the present wasted,
A draining of dregs that leaves the cup of life's new joys untasted."

Then, closing the book of old world dreams, I clasp it without misgiving,
Determined to dream of the past no more, but live for the coming living:
To plough the furrow and sow the seed, and bless myself and neighbour,
And make the world look bright once more, with the scattered gold of labour.

The hazy mist that hung in the sky, and baffled my sense of vision,
The fickle fancies that trooping came, and killed my soul's decision,
The want of purpose, of will and thought, the dreamy undulation,
That weakened every true impulse to kill the soul's stagnation.

The longing for things that had passed before, for joys that I craved to borrow;
The lingering look at the lifeless past, and want of thought for to-morrow;
All, all, had flown, and a newer life had taken root and flourished,
And drew its sap from the wasted source that idle fancies nourished.

"All labour is life," "All sloth is death," is written on earth and ocean,
And bright as the shining stars appear, they gather their light from motion,
They, onward and onward, for evermore go, for ever, and ever, and ever,
And show us the secret of endless life, is writ in the word "Endeavour!"

ONLY A DREAMER.

Only a dreamer, only a dreamer,
  Pass him by, pass him by;
Why should we trouble our heads about him?
  You and I.
Let the fool dream that the world wi alter,
  Get wiser and better, in rhythm an rhyme;
Come away Harry, come away, Wal ter,
  The world only moves at its own set time.

Keep to the pathway, keep to the pathway,
  It will do, it will do;
Why should we seek for newer and better?
  I and you.
Let the poor work out their own salvation,
  Get freer and better as best they may,
We will keep step with the bulk of the nation,
  Unmindful of those who may fail by the way.

There is no danger, there is no danger,
  Let him cry, let him cry;
Why should we trouble our heads about him?
  You and I.
Let the fool cherish his visioned to-morrow,
  And fill in his pictures with rhythm and rhyme,
Careless of grief, and careless of sorrow,
  The world only moves at its own set time.

List to the dreamer! List to the dreamer!
  Calling us back! calling us back!
In tones that are stirred by sudden danger:
  "Death on your track! death on your track!"
Swift as the wind, for your own salvation,
  Fly for your life, as best you may;
The dreamers of dreams are the kings of the nation,
  The scorned of the scorners of yesterday.

OVER A CENTURY.

The tide has receded and left her ashore,
  Was the thought that came rushing to me,
She will nevermore mingle with friends as of yore,
  She was fifty, and fifty, and three.
She had outlived her friends, she had outrun her time,
  And her skin was the colour of gold;
"I was once the May Queen," she would say, "in my prime;
  But I'm old, very old, very old."

She was dressed as she dressed, in the days that had gone,
  Though the fashion had long passed away,
And the little old dame, as she slowly walked on,
  No longer looked joyous and gay.
She had failed to return with the tide of Old Time,
  As backward and backward it rolled,
"I could dance like a fairy," she'd say, "in my prime;
  But I'm old, very old, very old."

An old friend once called her "a black-lettered tome
  With its parchment beshrivelled by Time,
That bids us prepare for the kingdom to come,
  In the midst of our glory and prime."
She'd a memory stored with the joys of passed days,
  That she treasured as though they were gold,
And would call back the words that had sounded her praise,
  And end with, "I'm old, very old."

She was fairly upright, though a little bit lame,
  Which but few would have seen as she passed;
You'd have thought that a picture had walked from its frame,
  Or a ghost had crept out of the past.
Every Sabbath, I'm told, she would journey to church,
  And count up her friends in the fold,
And glancing around at the graves from the porch,
  She would say, "I am old, very old."

It was hard to decide whether pleasure or pain
  Held her spirit most under control;
Though the song of her youth had been lost, the refrain
  Had been never crushed out of her soul.
She would fight her love battles all over once more,
  Till the pleasure thus won made her bold,
And would say when futurity troubled her sore,
  "I am old, very old, very old."

She was callous of days that had nothing to give,
  She was dead to all passing around;
In the memoried scenes of the past, she would live,
  And with fresh-woven flowers be crowned:
But the dream passed away, she the present would skip,
  And turn to the shepherd and fold,
And exclaim, as she passed Sorrow's cup to her lip,
  "I am old, very old, very old."

THE AFTERMATH.

ADDENDA TO "KIMBURTON."

1.—THE PLOUGHING MATCH.

There were parsons, and squires and farmers,
    And tradesmen from twenty miles round,
And beside them, their wives and their daughters,
    Like flowers besprinkled the ground;
Gay crocuses dressed out in yellow,
    And roses in crimson and red,
And a nosegay of merry wag-wantons,
    A-bobbing at Tom, Jack and Ned.

In the morning the weather looked doubtful,
    Umbrellas were thick in the crowd;
And the sun that had got a bit cur'us,
    Kept peeping from under a cloud:
Then he wentered a leetle bit furder,
    And thought he would see it outright,
Till the light and the warmth of his presence,
    Soon put all their vague fears to flight.

There were those who were chosen for judges,
    And horses and ploughs by the score;
With the band of the County Militia,
    And crowds of the poorest of poor.
And the music was grand—it was awful!
    It woke up the girls and the boys;
If you didn't get the right stuff for money,
    Egad! you got plenty of noise.

There was Jimmy who worked for old Trumper,
    And Jerry who toiled at "The Vatch,"
And a comrade called Sandy, a Scotchman,
    And five or six more in the match;
And among them, my neighbour, Dan Spicer,
    With furrows all over his brow,
Who had won full a score of such matches,
    By slicing the land with a plough.

Master Spicer was guided by knowledge,
    And did not make a splutter or boast,
Little Jimmy was nervously shaking,
    And felt that his chances were lost!

But the "Vatchman" was mighty valiant,
    And, as for the brawny-limbed Sco[t]
He was looking as fierce as a maggot
    And thought he could polish the l[ot]

Now we know there's a motive for things,
    For every deed that we do;
For every task undertaken,
    And sometimes, perchance, there [are] two:
It be honour, or greed, or ambition,
    But what I be going to prove,
Is that neither of these, nor a mixtur',
    Are equal to woman and love.

Little Jimmy who funked at the starting
    Had promised a cherry-cheeked lass,
He would marry, and set the bells ringing
    As soon as he'd saved up the brass.
And the light of her eye shone afore him,
    And marked where the furrow shoul[d] run,
And the share kept as true as an arrow,
    And that's how the battle was won.

In a week's time they gave out th[e] prizes,
    Ten guineas for brave little Jim,
It was not a big sum for the wealthy,
    But seemed like a fortune to him;
And the winner kept true to his promise,
    And married the lass straight away,
And the light of the blue eye that led him,
    Still keeps him from going astray.

—o—

2.—THE WIDOW'S LUCK.

She was what I should please to call gentle,
    She didn't have to rough it like we,
But she married Ned Painter, a carter,
    And Ned soon pegged out, d'yer see;
Then of course she was left a lorn widder,
    Had children? no; only jest one,
Who had reached two year old when they parted,
    And was learning to toddle and run.

THE AFTERMATH.

She lived in that little thatched cottage,
  That 'ere where them kids be at play;
That one, with the queer-fashioned gable,
  With winders a-looking this way:
She was there with the child that she worshipped,
  She struggled to live and to thrive,
But the queen bee arn't used to go hunting,
  And Poverty crept in the hive.

No, she wasn't them sort as go begging;
  The neighbours a-living next door,
Though a little bit puzzled about her,
  Didn't dream she was starvingly poor.
You see, sir, she always looked tidy,
  And that carried off a good deal,
And the poor folk who doesn't look dirty,
  Bean't thought to be wanting a meal.

It was just when the game was nigh over,
  That Fortune gave heed to her prayer,
When the light of hope sank in the socket,
  And nothing remained but despair;
It was then, like an angel o' mercy,
  A stranger was seen by her side,
Just returned from a trip on the ocean,
  Who wanted to make her his bride.

"That boy," said he, "won't make no diff'rence,
  Just hand the lad over to me,"
And, in less than a minute, that sailor,
  Was dancing young Ned on his knee,
"We be messmates, yer see, in an instant,
  Come, come, lass, leap into the boat;
He is wanted to balance the vessel,
  And help me to keep her afloat."

Now, yer see, sir, they wasn't like strangers,
  They know'd one another afore;
They were schoolmates and playmates, and neighbours,
  And, I fancies, a little bit more.
Till a sort of a tiff rose atween 'em,
  He started to sea, right away,
And the news came, the vessel he sailed in,
  Had sunk in a very queer way.

She was bound to the coast of Australey,
  And the truth of it be jest this 'ere,
There was summat about that ship's captain
  That looked, well, a leetle bit queer.

Now, I don't know what judges may think on't,
  Or juries; but this be the tale,
But I fancies the verdict be "guilty,"
  Ay, "guilty," as safe as the mail.

When the vessel was lying in harbour,
  And most of the crew had got leave,
It was said as the water ran in her,
  As though she was made like a sieve,
Then she canted, and went to the bottom,
  And there she be still, I dare say,
When the captain, the only one in her,
  Swam off to the shore, right away.

Then the shipmates got hard up in Sydney,
  For wanting of summat to do,
When, at length, that 'ere fearful gold fever
  Got hold of the most of the crew.
Then the lover she jilted, Tom Fowler,
  Soon hit on a rare lucky find,
And the first thought he had was to share it
  With her he had left far behind.

'Twas a slice of good luck for the widder,
  Her heart fairly bubbled with joy,
She had found in her earliest lover
  A father to care for her boy;
He was happy, indeed, sir, so happy,
  Oh, yes, there's one more in the fold,
Little Tom, that his dad calls his bos'n,
  And now, sir, my story be told.

As for Tom, that's her husband, God bless him,
  He says he be anchored on shore,
And he calls his snug home, a trim vessel,
  And uses sich words by the score.
But, yer know it's the way with them sailors,
  They don't speak a langwidge like we,
It be more nor a half on it forren,
  And seems jest like nonsense to me.

—o—

3.—A LAY SARMINT.

I be only a yokel, and not a bit clever,
  And measter's a notion he's got I dirt cheap,
But I knows a bit more than he thinks, howsomever,
  And I fancies he arn't canght a weasel asleep.
I might ha' worked harder, if that brought a livin',
  Ay, worked wi' a will, if I'd been fairly paid ;
But fourpence for tuppence, why, dang it! that's givin',—
  That can't be the style in which fortunes be made.

Our pearson may prach about duty to measter,
  But why don't he talk of his duty to I ?
The stuff in his sarmints don't make I work feaster,
  And to say it be Scriptur's a tarnation lie.
Every horse in the steable be far better treated
  Than we chaps who toil at the spade or the plough,
It's a falsehood to say we were born to be cheated,
  But there arn't many fools to believe in that now.

They've bin payin' for quarts, and have bin gettin' punchins,
  But I'm blarmed if they'll get any more out o' me ;
If my work be worth dinners, it ain't paid by lunchins,
  So I jest takes the balance to make things agree.
While there's game in the wood, and fish in the river,
  That Nature has put there, I'll never go short,
It be plunderin' no man to take from the giver,
  The food that be wasted for pleasure and sport.

There be chaps that be gone from Ol[d] land for ever,
  Who couldn't stand the porrige th[ey get] over here ;
And meas[t]er now says they were a[ll] clever,
  And be always lamentin' their loss [with a] tear.
He says we arn't in it wi' them chap[s for] workin',
  And that all honest industry's b[een done] away,
That all we be good for be skulkin[' and] shirkin',
  Then why didn't he 'tice sich good [peo]ple to stay ?

He be got what he axed for, and ough[t not] to grumble,
  It be wrong to complain when you [get] what you seek ;
When here, all they got was a lean bon[e to] fumble,
  They couldn't fill their stomicks on bob a week.
They didn't like the workus to spend th[eir] last days in,
  They didn't want their children to star[ve] and to die,
So they bolted, God bless 'em, and [our] measter's praises
  Won't tempt 'em from comfort and plen[ty] to fly.

Let them preach to the farmers 'bout bein[g] contented,
  For I'm blessed if they'll get sich co[n]tent out o' me,
They may put up the price of the cottag[e] I've rented,
  And lop off my garden as close as [a] tree.
They may steal all the waste land, th[e] roadside and common,
  And strip all below them till each [be] quite bare ;
But God has entrusted to me my ol[d] woman,
  And by fair means or foul in God's riche[s] we'll share.

e there's I, and there's Bill Stokes,
  my neighbour,
 a score of good men who are honest
  and true,
 have made the earth laugh in a harvest by labour,
 d gathered the grass when besprinkled
  with dew.
 lon't mean to give lots of labour for
  nuffin',
 farmers, nor landlords, nor any sich
  folk;
 fine birds in future must find their
  own stuffin',
 nd we poor chaps 'll see how they stu-
  mick the joke,

 he rent be too high, they must charge a
  bit lower,
 nd if tythings be burthens, we'll sweep
  'em away,
 ere be plenty o' wealth in the sunshine
  and shower,
 \nd labour must tempt it to cuddle the
  clay.
  must make findin's keepin's, and starve
  out the varmints,
 And give to the giver who's labour to
  give;
  who fights with the cold shall be clad
  in warm garmints,
 And the life spent in giving shall learn
  how to live.

—o—

4.—A TALE OF A DOG.

 a this thick-peopled land, it is strange
  that a soul
 hould be found with no mortal with whom
  to condole,
 ut it's true as it's strange, that, on this
  crowded shore,
 've seen, in my time, well, a thousand or
  more,
  Who could not boast a friend
  Who would give or would lend.
 here are cravings in nature that nothing
  can hide,
 hey may ebb, they may flow, with the
  neap or spring tide,
 ut such wants will make themselves felt
  till supplied?

If you dare doubt the fact, I will instantly
  prove
That a man craves for friendship, and
  woman for love,
And will take to a dog, a cat, or a bird,
(Which act, there are those who call, well,
  absurd.)
  But the gnawings endured,
  May, in part, be thus cured,
By the love of a cat, or a dog, or the
  song,
Which a linnet or goldfinch will pipe all
  day long.
Now Miss Jenny Macfoodle, though cold as
  a frog,
Was remarkably fond of a cross-tempered
  dog,
Who would snarl, seize and worry the
  folks who passed by,
And take a piece out of their calves on the
  sly.
This unsocial brute was as ugly as sin,
Both his forelegs were twisted, the knees
  turning in,
And its habits were filthy, nor washing
  nor scrubbing
Was half so much wanted as constantly
  drubbing;
But, of all his great faults, there were none
  to compare
With the length of his tail, his coat and
  his ear.
  "I will have his tail lopped,
  And his ears shall be cropped,
  The dear little poodle,"
  Said Jenny Macfoodle.
Then she called on a very close neighbour,
  called Giles,
And plied him with soft words, and good-
  natured smiles,
To cut her dog's tail off, and clip both his
  ears,
And, when he refused, she tried a few
  tears.
"I will hold him," said he, "that's the
  most I can do;
But the chopping, dear lady, I must leave
  to you!"
Now Giles, I may say, without any asper-
  sion,
To this dog, of all dogs, had a mortal aver-
  sion.
  "The block is quite ready,"
  Said he, "hold him steady!"

Then down came the chopper,
  Or cleaver—a whopper!
The aim of the maiden was doubtlessly true,
But, from some cause, the dog was cut clean in two!
  Either Giles was unsteady,
  Or, maybe, too ready,
Or, as was proclaimed by the single beholder,
"He hated the brute, and its owner, and sold her."
But Giles, who was one of the cucumber sort,
Cried, "Blarm me! Miss Jenny! you've cut his tail short!"

—o—

5.—THE FARM-YARD NIGHTINGALE.

Oh, yes, he be fond of his donkey,
  Very fond o' the brute, I be told;
But, you see, for the work he be doin',
  The creeter be gittin' too old;
He can't do a deal o' hard labour,
  And can't step along over quick,
And Jemmy, who can't buy no fodder,
  In kindness, oft gives him the stick.

Yes, lib'ral in all of his actions,
  "Don't spare it?" Not he, take my word,
When hit, his old moke starts a-singin',
  "His tongue be a leetle bit furred."
Well, yes, 'tis a leetle bit gratey,
  "Good chest notes?" No; right from the throat,
He only j st wants a white weskit,
  White choker, and swaller-tail coat.

He'd draw a few pounds, I'm a-thinkin',
  "If harnessed," I said in a joke,
"He has drawn many pounds," said he, winkin',
  "Afore his old bellus got broke."
There! listen! there's music! my pippin,
  There's fortunes for Harris or Gye,
Bass, baritone, tenor, and treble,
  There, jest tell me how's that for high?

"He sticks up his back," said I, sm
  "Bean't graceful, and don't ma bow,"
Why, bless me, you don't think him man,
  He's got as much grace as a cow.
I own he bean't much of an actor,
  But that comes by practice, I 'spose
He's a nat'ral sort of a singer,
  The BOUGH will be there, when it gro

"Not tender?" well, I calls it tender,
  At times, too, it's pretty and sweet;
It's summat musicians could dine off,
  As tender as steak when it's beat;
You don't like the strain; well, don't l it,
  Nor twist that he gives to his jaw;
The fust, be all nonsense, my pippin,
  THE STRAIN BE THE THING THAT WII DRAW!

—o—

6.—A SECOND SKETCH OF KIMBURTON.

As you climb up the deep-rutted roadwa
  And gaze from the top of the hill,
You see a bright stream in the valley,
  And, stretching across it, a mill;
Then a church that is covered with ivy,
  Whose spire points up to the sky,
With a huge brazen bird perched upon it,
  That always seems going to fly.

On one side are very high mountains,
  That start from a wide-stretching moor,
Adjoining a bit of a common,
  That hasn't been filched from the poor.
On the other an old-fashioned homestead.
  And, close by, the squire's estate,
Surrounded by moss-covered palings,
  And reached by a large iron gate.

At its side, stands the village, Kimburton,
  A cluster of broken-down sheds,
That one would imagine a strong wind
  Would scatter and tear into shreds.
They are built in the old-fashioned mud style,
  And let in the wind and the rain,
Roofed in with dry reeds from the marshes,
  And mapped out with many a stain.

[re] folks that are fond of Kimburton,
[heart]-strings bound fast to the place,
[a] smile peeping over each wrinkle
[whene]ver you look in their face.
[A]re some like the bird on its steeple,
[That] always seems ready to fly;
[So]me whose last efforts were wasted
[In cr]ossing its threshold to die.

[There] is one poor old man in a cottage,
[Who] has suffered for many a day,
[F]eels the delights of his boyhood,
[Gro]w greener as life ebbs away;
[A] child lying sick in its cradle,
[Whose] heart never felt a full throb,
[Is] known through the length of the village
[A]s "Lavender's poor little Bob."

[The]re's a cripple who limps upon crutches,
[A] sailor who's been to the wars,
[A] proud-looking, grey-bearded soldier,
[W]hose body is covered with scars;
[And] a miller, a sexton, a baker,
[W]ith one or two farmers about,
[And] a wheelwright, a smith, and a grocer,
[A]nd publican merry and stout.

[The]re's a postman, who brings all the letters,
[A]nd a chap who drives in with the mail,
[A keeper], some helps, a few poachers,
[W]ho spend half their lifetime in jail:
[And], of course, there's the fool of the village,
[W]hom boys never see but they tease;
[Dre]ssed up in an old pair of breeches,
[A] trifle too long at the knees.

[The]re's a squire, a doctor, a parson,
[A] brotherly, freemason band,
[An]d each holds a third of the village
[C]lutched tight in the palm of his hand.
[An]d then, horny-handed and sunburnt,
[A] thousand of toilers or so,
[W]ho live on the skirts of the common,
[O]r linger in Ginbottle Row.

[I'v]e toiled many years in Kimburton,
[A]nd struggled till heartsick and grey,
[And] the promise that cheered me in springtime,
[H]as flown with its sunshine away.

Yet, still, there's no place in the wide world,
  To which I'd more readily fly,
Than the valley where Kimburton steeple
  Climbs over the hills to the sky.

—o—

7.—SWAPPING HORSES.

Now, I daresay you'll think I am joking
  When I tell yer this bit of a tale,
But I 'sure yer it's true, my good measters,
  As that I be fond of good ale.
And to give yer a proof that I likes it,
  Afore I commences to start,
I axes if any will try me
  By standin' a pint or a quart.

That's good! bitin' halves only spiles it,
  Yer see I were mortally dry,
And yer see there be none at the bottom
  To moisten the foot of a fly.
Well, what if there bean't a drain in it,
  I think I have proved it quite clear,
That if there ain't nought in the story,
  Old Michael be fond of his beer.

Yer know'd our Old Dobbin well, didn't yer?
  As decent a horse as yer'd find;
He was never afraid of the collar,
  Though a leetle bit touched in the wind;
He had got a white star on the forehead,
  His fetlocks were spotted with snow,
He was—well, I couldn't call him handsome,
  And, in course, at his age, a bit slow.

Yes, that's 'ow it was that the measter
  Had tuk a dislike to the horse;
But I loved it, and used for to tell him
  He could easy get one as was wus;
But measter was always bit stubborn,
  And liked for to have his own way,
And, taking Old Dobbin to Lunnun,
  He, what I calls, guv'd him away.

He swapped him away for another,
  Old Dobbin, and five pounds to boot,
For a reg'lar cross-tempered gibber—
  I never cum'd near sich a brute;
He had smashed up our measter's new barrer,
  And tore down the manger and rack,
But the brute being bought of a stranger
  There was no chance of sending him back.

HISTORICAL AND OTHER POEMS
RELATING TO
UXBRIDGE AND ITS NEIGHBOURHOOD.

THE TREATY OF UXBRIDGE.

Withering leaves lay scattered around,
Stretched by the wind on the cold clay ground;
Shrivelled and sapless, black and red,
Trampled and sodden, cold and dead.
On many a now historic plain,
The storm of strife had its thousands slain,
And friend and foe commingling lay,
Like soddened leaves on the cold, cold clay.

Good men prayed the storm might cease,
Wise men sighed for the reign of Peace,
And anxious mothers, near and far,
Watched for a turn in the tide of war.
Gay, joyous hearts that once beat high,
Embittered, answered sigh with sigh,
And bruisèd souls in cries of pain,
Pleaded for peace, and pleaded in vain.

By many a scattered ingle side,
Tears were shed for the household pride,
And prayer and sigh, and sigh and prayer,
Rose side by side on the startled air:
And widowed wives, and ruined homes,
And new-spilt blood, and crowded tombs,
Pleaded for Peace, and Hope ruled high,
That the voice of Despair had reached the sky.

There's a sudden lull, only whispers are heard
A small still voice by the breath of Peace stirred,
And warriors resting, are dreaming once more
Of children they love and wives they adore.
Around each well-known tavern site,
Gossips are gathering, left and right,
The partizans of nation and king,
Like bees in clusters are mustering.

Down where the shires are cut asunder,
And the silvery Colne doth for evermore wander,
Busy men toil by night and by day,
To make the Council Chamber gay;
And now the tables and chairs are set,
And the pick of the royal cabinet
Are face to face with the Nestors sent
From the nation's chosen parliament.

Many a scholarly penman's scroll
On the crimson cloth the clerks unroll,
And ears are quickened to catch the word
That will sharpen or shiver the crusted sword.
Cordial greetings come thick and fast,
And the Pisgah of Peace seems reached at last,
And the dark black clouds of yesterday
Seem passing away, passing away.

Days roll on, and Hope and Fear
Alternate come and disappear,
And Love, the zealot, is preaching hard by,
Lifting his hands to the storm-cast sky,
And shouting aloud, "My God! your God!
Is thirsting anew for human blood,"
And the same straight lines that never meet,
Divide the council, the town and street.

Once more the councillors meet in vain
To wrangle and so depart again,
And the voice of the preacher is heard afar,
Shouting aloud for God and War,
And mass is called that men may pray
For the nation's sins to be washed away;
That peaceful blessings like summer rain
May fall on this dear old land again.

But, alas! for their prayers, the ways of men,
Have turned the land to a tiger's den,
And stubborn pride, and hate and fear,
Assert their presence everywhere.
The teeth of the dragon are broadly sown
Their evil fibres have struck and grown,

Till Love, like corn, where bind-weeds spread,
Borne down to earth, lies cankered and dead.

"My bond, my bond," the King has cried,
"My kingly rights whate'er betide;
The power of sceptre, power of crown
To rule my slaves and keep men down."
"Our rights," the opposition cry,
"For which we've sworn to live or die;
Our rights to fill the trust we hold
By blood-won charters manifold."

"The rights of the King are the rights of God!"
"The rights of the people are sealed with blood!"
"No man from his King has the right to recede."
"We won it by charter at Runnymede!"
"The form of religion, the King must choose!"
"Never while men have souls to loose!"
"'Tis the King's to take, not yours to give!"
"Where slaves exist; not where men live!"

Heavily burthened with care and woe,
Each friend of peace moves to and fro,
With never a hope to give him rest,
Or banish the fear that builds its nest
In the heart of the watcher who watches in vain
For Peace long fled, to return again;
For a break in the dense, dark clouds above,
That curtain the earth from the dawn of love.

In the Council Hall not a word is spent
By the agents of King or parliament;
Not a plea advanced but hate is stirred;
Not a note is struck but a discord heard;
And the dissolution, drawing nigh,
Will close in the solemn mockery,
Of striving to bridge a divided land
With planks of speech on piles of sand.

On the unripe sheaf, the thresher's flail
Is vainly spent, and the empty tale*
Standing beside the bruisèd reeds
That stubbornly retain their seeds,
With open mouth seems wondering
That labour unstinted so little doth bring.
Threshers of sheaves refusing to yield,
The laws of reason are unrepealed.

Threshers of sheaves in the wainscoted hall,
Green and wet and mouldering all,
The measure is empty, your labour in vain,
The straw is bruised, but the coveted grain
Is wanted still; go back and rest,
Both cause and failure manifest;
The gathering time had not yet come
When you raised the cry of "Harvest Home."

* Tale, a measure.

—o—

YE WOXBRUGGE TOLLE RIOT.
(1631.)

Gather ye tolle, gather ye tolle,
Swell up ye Countesse's ryche rente rolle,
Lette no beaste pass to market or faire,
Nor quarterre of corne be planted there
    Withouten ye tolle.

"An antiente righte (or an antiente wrong)
Confirmeth such tolle toe ye Countesse belonge,"
Sayd her ladyshippe's steward, Rychard Lee,
"Forgather ye tolle and bringe yt to me;
    Gather ye tolle."

Is yt ye winde a-blowing uppe rayne,
A gentil gale or a hurricane,
Or is yt ye voice of an angered soule,
That careth noughte for ye Countesse's rolle,
    Disputing ye tolle?

Baker, ye Burgesse, and Baker, ye clerke,
Guarded with servantes, with pystol and dirke,
Are, bearding ye justice, Sir Rychard Carr,
Defiantly waging a wordy war;
    Claiming ye tolle.

Now they have mounted ye granerie stair,
Daring ye stewarde toe enter there;

Daring ye justice standing neare,
Atte hys own life-peryl toe interfere,
    Or take ye tolle.

Ye proclamacyon ys reade aloude,
In ye myddle of ye surgyng crowde,
But ye constable's voice, though stout and strong,
Ys drowned by ye shoutes of ye rabble throng,
    Disputing ye tolle.

Foster and Priest, two serving men,
Are crowching like s'aves in a tiger's denne,
With strycken courage and quivering nerve,
Lackynge ye power ye Countesse to serve,
    To seize ye tolle.

Mangled and torn, yn sorre dismaye
Ye Countesse's servantes are driven away,
And ye goude Sir Knighte and hys henchman true —
Are met by ye scome of ye rabble crew,
    Who seize ye tolle.

But, alas! for ye victors who won ye day,
And chaced ye Justice in feare away,
And, alas! for those who cheered them on,
And cried "Huzza! for ye victorie wonne,"
    And " Guarde ye tolle."

Alas! for ye flashes of merriemente,
And ye boastyng roysteryng heart contente,
For ye rollycking, jovial, loude-mouthed songe,
Trolled bye a score of voices strong,
    Anent ye tolle.

For ye vallyante toastes, alas! alas!
That rounde ye boarde so merrilie pass,
For emptie flagon and wine-cuppe dry,
And shoutes that rende ye midnight sky;
    "Stand by ye tolle!"

Alas! and alack! for ye visions brighte,
That hover around ye Burgesse at night,
For dreams that nothing but victorie telle,
And ye firste faint flushe of morn will dispel.
    Anent ye tolle.

Countesse and Stewarde in council have met,
To confer with ye baffled Baronet,
And warrantes and charges are speedilie drawn,
And affidavits made and sworne
    To claym ye tolle.

Ring out, ring out! ye merrie bells,
Your marriage cadences and swells,
"Ring out ye olde, ring yn ye newe,"
Ring out ye hatred discord drewe,
Ring out for ye victor who harbours noe strife,
Ring for ye Countesse, Lord Derby's wife;
Ring out and swell ye fair renowne,
Of those who foughte for ye goude olde town,
    And ye market tolle.

— o —

THE LYNCH MARTYRS.
(1555.)

'Twas in the glorious autumn time,
  The flowers were in full blossom,
And golden sheaves and harvest rows
  Were resting on earth's bosom;
And the burning sun was overhead,
  The boughs with ripe fruit bending,
And the song of the lark from the bright blue sky
  On rays of light descending.

Over the town the blue heavens stretched,
  Over the bordering river,
Over the lowlands that margin the Colne,
  That journeys on for ever;
Over the park and the heather land,
  Over the fen-fields valley,
Where willows that sprout from the dark ditch side
  Form into a leafy alley.

The neighbours were gathered together in crowds
  Far away from the outlying places,
In market and store and neighbouring inns,
  Were crowded familiar faces.
  And many a stranger from east and west,
And north and south did journey,
As though the day had been set apart
  For feasting, fair or tourney.

The clock struck one, and the market place,
  Rang out with shouts and screeching.

And in their midst a holy friar
  With sweaty face was preaching;
And from the windows ranging round,
  Were seen a hundred faces,
Of souls that cheered the preacher on
  With weird and wild grimaces.

But presently from a neighbouring farm,
  Four bullocks were seen to drag on,
A load of bushes and undergrowth,
  On a cumbrous, creaking wagon;
And, loudly swelling, a wild hurrah,
  Stopped preaching and ballad singing,
And all the bells in the steepled church,
  Hard by were set a-ringing.

Down, down the lane to the old Lynch Green,
  The crowds go shouting and pushing;
From Cowley, Drayton, and all around,
  A sister stream came rushing,
Of young and old, of rich and poor,
  In the bright sunshiny weather,
With thirsty eyes for the sacrifice
  That had brought them altogether.

A hole was dug in the clayey soil,
  A stout post thrust in after,
And every step was a signal good
  For ribald jest and laughter,
And the sight of bramble, and beech and fir,
  With resin and pitch besprinkled,
Lit up the faces of all around,
  No matter how smooth or wrinkled.

The stack's now raised and for places round,
  The maddened crowd are fighting;
The manacled victim is close at hand,
  And the match is ready for lighting;
Then the shout was heard "Make way! make way!"
  And obeyed by the crowd assembled,
And pale but undauntless, the martyr comes,
  Who neither shook nor trembled.

He has not a fear to damp his soul,
  He has pity for each rude scoffer;
He is there to die as he lived for truth,
  To triumph and not to suffer!
He is there to seal with his warm red blood,
  The gospel, the mind's conceiving,
The only thing in the wide wide world,
  That honest men believe in.

There was nought of the smooth-faced hypocrite,
  Who basks in the reigning fashion,
His hands for the fetters, if Fate's decree—
  His bare back to ply the lash on;
His limbs for the rack, his foot for the boot,
  His body for flames if wanting,
Unblenched, untouched, unshook, intact,
  No canting nor recanting.

The martyr fixed and the match ablaze,
  And the fiend with the pitchfork draggling,
To bring together each burning bush
  That parted bonds leave straggling;
And now the light to the pile is raised,
  And the flame is mounting higher,
And now and now for the crucial test,
  The proving of gold by fire.

Higher and higher, still it burns,
  The sticks are crackling round him,
But there in the midst, is the martyr still
  With the holiness that crowned him;
There, in the midst, with his hands upraised,
  There while the bells are ringing,
Telling the truth as revealed to him,
  And meeting Death with singing.

Though arms are stripped of all their flesh,
  And nether limbs consuming,
He shouts aloud, to the gathered crowd,
  Of the triumph that is coming;
He prays to God, to Freedom's God,
  To cool his wrath and anger,
And lead the priest-led into paths,
  That truth keeps clear of danger.

Again he has started to sing aloud,
  Great God, for his strength bepraising,
And his withering arms are heavenward stretched,
  'Mid resinous brushwood blazing;
And around the portals of heaven, thrown back,
  The crowding angels linger,
Watching and waiting, expectantly,
  To catch the soul of the singer.

'Tis over now; his life has sped,
  All fleshly ties have parted,
But upward, upward, purified,
  The living soul has started;

And cheated bigots are tricked once more,
  Confounded, mocked, and baffled ;
'Tis ever thus, the soul they'd kill,
  Is freed by fire and scaffold.

It reeks not of the fagot thrown,
  It fears no earthly terror,
It lives in heaven to lead the world,
  From tangled paths of error ;
It pleads for man to Freedom's God,
  It stirs each living nation,
And through his blood who died that day,
  We living, owe salvation.

Over the town the black clouds fall,
  Over the burning embers,
Over the church of Saint Margaret,
  And over its listening members.
But to-morrow the darkness will slink away,
  Wherever the sunlight rushes,
And faces that wore the frown of hate
  Shall burn with their own hot blushes.

The sun-light of Love has quenched the flames
  That rival creeds long nurtured,
And banished the crimson stains that marked
  How men in hate were tortured ;
And fears that held men's minds in thrall
  And mental chains that bound them,
Have melted away in the light of love
  And the glow of warmth around them.

—o—

THE MOUND ON THE MOOR.

It was only a mound of heaped-up earth—
  Of mould and clay ;
And, thought to be of nothing worth,
  They swept it away :
Swept it away, for ever and ever,
The mound that for ages had stood by the river.

Little they knew, and little they cared,
  Why it was raised,
And when they heard what love it shared,
  They stood amazed,
And said, " Why—for ever,
  Should a mound encumber the field by the river?

Its history no one knows—can know—
  That's past and gone ;
It had worn its thousand crowns of snow—
  Silent ! alone ;
Out in the cold, without a shiver,
Time was nought to the mound by the river.

It reared no golden crops of corn,
  'Twas profitless !
But yet a thought, however born,
  May cheer and bless,
And thought on thought, grow ever and ever,
Out of the mound that stood by the river.

But the hidden-memory mound of mould
  Is now effaced,
This landmark of the men of old
  Long, long, erased.
Over the land you may wander for ever,
And find no trace of the mound by the river.

No mythical story of Launcelot,
  Or Druid creed,
Had clung to that old world sacred spot,
  And shed its seed,
Living on for ever and ever,
Growing out of that mound by the river.

No story of gods or godlike men,
  No wizard's tale,
Nought of Sir Valance or Vivien,
  Or holy grail ;
'Twas only a mound no storm could shiver
That stood beside the flowing river.

'Twas a page of history none could read,
  Standing alone,
The text of some startling old world deed
  With no key-stone ;
A memory lost, gone back to the giver,
A pile of dust by the on-flowing river.

Or was it a mound to cover the dead —
  A resting place ?
A Gethsemane where tears were shed
  By an ancient race ?
Alas ! the truth has perished for ever,
Like the scattered mound by the on-flowing river.

Or was it a place for tourney or strife —
  Or battlement?
Where many a brave in lusty life
  His last bolt spent ?
When, sinking to rest with empty quiver
He waits for his Judge by the banks of the river?

Or was it the work of Roman or Dane,
  Of plundering might?
Or was it planned for some Saxon thane
  Or mystic rite?
Vainly we ask, for never, never,
Will the answer come from the mound by
    the river.

No whispering wraith, or babbling ghost,
  Has deigned to stay;
The earth-mound scattered—its purpose
    lost—
  Blotted away;
Blotted away, for ever, and ever,
  The old-world mound by the on-flowing
    river.

—o—

THE HISTORY OF GERARD CROSS.

He was a little CROSS when he was born!
  But that was natural, considering his
    paternity;
His name was CROSS, this name in fact
    was worn
  By Mr. CROSS and all the CROSS fraternity.
The CROSSES of mankind are somewhat
    old,
  I've traced them back to that old gal,
    Ann Tiquity!
In truth, by some historians we're told
  The CROSSES sprang from Mother Eve's
    Iniquity.

Young Gerard CROSS, a COMMONER, no
    doubt,
  Was born in Bucks., just two days before Sunday,
And being CROSS, began to bawl and
    shout,
  And make his first noise in the world
    on Hot CROSS Bun day.
Young Gerard CROSS, I here my tale renew,
  Displayed a love for driving and for
    horses,
And oft from school this naughty boy
    withdrew,
  Leaving his fellows with their pencilled
    CROSSES.

He grew a-pace, and soon became a man,
  Made love in haste, repented at his
    leisure;
A CROSS in love upset his little plan,
  Of CROSSES, Gerard CROSS had more
    than measure.
He then turned farmer! but he didn't
    succeed,
  Each CROSS he had increased his many
    losses,
So being poor, and very much IN-KNEED,
  He started selling jams, and these were
    CROSS's!

The CROSS-bred cattle proved a failure
    quite,
  "The Bull" of Gerard Cross a failure
    utter;
His last cow died one cold and frosty night,
  And long before he hadn't any BUTTER!
Then Gerard, CROSS, oppressed and filled
    with woe,
  For wedded happiness began to hunger,
And so impatient did young Gerard
    grow,
  He courted two, Miss LINES and Mistress YOUNGER.

The last-named lady had been married
    twice,
  Was old, though YOUNGER by her second marriage,
The former was a lady, spruce and nice,
  And being young, of course, she KEPT
    HER CARRIAGE!
Oh! pickles! CROSS's pickles! and real
    jam!
  A fool alone would hesitate much
    longer,"
Now take this for a regular funnigram,
  He, taking LINES, left Mistress
    YOUNGER YOUNGER.

With speed increased, the passing years
    now fly,
  And little children round his knees are
    clustered,
The light of love is seen in Gerard's eye,
  He knows no condiment like CROSS's
    MUSTERED.
And little CROSSES springing from his
    LINES!
  Were never heard to cry or eke to
    blubber,
They go upon the common, if it shines,
  Or else he wipes them out with India
    rubber!

—o—

THE BATTLE OF BULSTRODE IN 1066.
"THE CAMP OF REFUGE."

Traces of war, traces of war,
Flat broad plain, with lines of scar,
  Encircling round.
Despite of centuries passed away,
The scar, like a moat, may be seen to-day—
  A fresh green wound.

I would that Tradition had more to tell
Of those who met, who fought, who fell,
Of those who followed, of those who led,
And the right and wrong for which they bled,
And all the strange, strange history
That Time has left a mystery !
No spark of light can now be caught ;
To show us how, or why men fought ;
What language owned their battle cries,
What was, what not, the coveted prize,
We wander o'er the hills and dells,
And all we know, Tradition tells.

Traces of war, traces of war,
Flat broad camp, with lines of scar,
  Encircling round ;
Gnarled oak trees that were born of eld,
Gnarled oak trees that a storm has felled,
  Stretched on the ground ;
Vainly to thee, we in darkness cry,
To clear away the mystery.

Was it here the Ancient Briton stood,
And bartered for freedom his warm heart blood ?
Or here that the conquering Roman hurled,
The javelin that shook the world ?
We thought in our pictured extremity,
We rested ourselves 'neath an ancient tree
That had waved its wide spread branches o'er
The camp for a thousand years or more.
And while so resting, this story heard
From the whispering leaves that the wind had stirred :

"When Hastings' fight was fought and won,
  And Harold lay with the dead ;
When the strife was o'er, and the deed was done,
  And the moon on its course had sped;
On a distant spot a gathered host
  Took counsel of what to do.
'We cannot fight ! the battle's lost ;
  They are many, and we are few.'

"So spoke the lips of an elderman,
  Fresh, flushed from the heated fray,
To comrades weary, and dazed, and wan,
  On the night of that fearful day.
To men whose pride no longer concealed,
  The pluck and strength of the foe ;
Brave men who marched to the battle-field,
  As men to a feast would go.

And the eldermen, who counsel gave,
Was no mean coward or sneaking knave ;
But true as steel ; from a foremost post
He had seen the battle won and lost ;
And the little strength that had not sped,
He wisely saw should be husbanded,
' Build Camps of Refuge all over the land,
And strengthen yourselves for another stand,
Your weakness cannot resist the sea
That rushes on so furiously.
The elder who spoke was Shobbington,
A Saxon chief who had led them on,
A brave who had learned from the deadly yew,
To yield to force, and yet be true;
In the pathless wilds of Lincolnshire,
Where Ely lifts its lofty spire,
On the broad flat plain from which I spring,
In the midst of heather, and fern, and ling,
Such camps were built, and how they stood
The assault of foemen was writ in blood.
But Time has washed the stain away,
And Tradition who saw not the bloody fray,
With weakened memory, has failed to tell,
How Shobbington, covered with glory, fell,
And the Camp of Refuge was stormed and ta'en,
When Shobbington kissed the gory plain."

The wind was hushed, and each whispering leaf
  Grew suddenly still,
But, anon, the wind, like a blustering thief,
  Swept over the hill,

And the leaves began to chatter once more
Of the brav s who fought in the days of yore.

"It was here," said they, "that the Saxon host
Who had fought in Hastings' fight and lost,
Being rid of their fears, together met,
To declare there was life in the good cause yet.
It was here, 'neath my branches, that Shobbington,
Planned out the camp we are resting on,
And here where he gave to each chief command
And prepared for his last and final stand.
'Go, you, Sir Ralph, to the western side,
And with your bowmen stem the tide,
And you, brave Pilcher of Foulmere go,
To the eastern bank and face the foe,
And Pinder of Woxbrigge, hie thee forth
And face the strangers from the north,
And, Friar of Chalefond, stand by me,
And worry the foe from bush and tree.'
Then he told off a thousand men or more,
To hold the water springs secure,
And to baffle Time, and to check the foe,
Bade a hundred men of Ruislip go
And make a fort of every tree
That stood 'tween the Camp and Hedgerley,
And men to watch, and men to guard,
The stream that runs through Iver's Ford,
'But pressed,' cried the Saxon, ' Nettleton,
Fall back and make for the boulder stone
That marks the turn in the winding way,
And prepare to die, or hold them at bay,
Till I can send to your relief
A few score men with their chosen chief.
Wamba of Stoke, and Gurth of Penn,
And trusty Hal of Missenden,
Gather your forces, and take your stand
On some fitting spot on the table land,
And calmly watch the course of the fray,
And strengthen those who by chance give way.'"

The winds then ceased, and so again
The thread of the story was broken in twain,
But stirred afresh by a blast more rude,
The whispering leaves their tale renewed :

"In the depth of a dark November night,
When I was in my prime,
The Normans swarmed from left to right—
Swarth braves from a distant clime ;
And, passing on, through Hedgerley,
I heard their ringing cheer,
As, one by one, their startled foes
Fell backward to the rear.

"I saw them gather in yonder vale,
And, shoulder to shoulder, climb
'Mid heather and bracken that bent to the gale
In the brave and olden time ;
And I saw the arrows go hurtling by
From the chasm that yawned at m feet,
And the stricken foe in terror fly,
For safety in retreat.

"Then again I saw the foe advance,
De Burgh was leading them on,
And 'Throw not an arrow away on chance,'
Was the cry of Shobbington.
Then 'Now's your time ; take aim and true,
And be sure each shot will tell ;'
And a crowd of angry arrows flew
And a thousand foemen fell.

"But wave on wave swept the brow of the hill,
And, ere the day was spent,
Though thousands were lying cold and still,
Yet thousands more were sent.
And the last of the Saxons, who, watching, stood,
Had long been called away
To resist the countless multitude,—
To keep the foe at bay.

"The arrows sped were no longer true,
The Saxon thews unstrung,
And the blunted spears the defenders threw
No longer whistled or sung ;
When Shobbington saw the fight was lost,
And, rushing to meet the tide,
To right, to left, his battle axe tossed,
And cumbered the steep hill side!

"Right and left, and left and right,
  Onward, and onward he goes,
Striking with all his main and might,
  And strewing his path with foes ;
A mower of men, with swathes of dead,
  Marking the way he trod,
Braves whom the brave De Burgh had led,
  Bathed in their own warm blood.

" Calling on Harold and all the dead,
All who in battle for home had bled,
All who had fought, and fighting, fell,
On earth and sky, on heaven and hell !
Right and left, and left and right,
Dashing to death with a giant's might ;
Seeing no danger, fired with wrath,
Dying and mangled choking his path,
'Tis a glorious, terrible night to see,
A soul on fire with bravery."

Softer and softer, the whispers ran,
  And softer and softer still,
And all I could gather was, " This brave man
  Lies buried under the hill ;
With good Sir Ralph, and Nettleton,
  And Wamba, and Gurth of Penn,
And, side by side, by the gateway stone,
  The Pinder and all his men.
And many a score in the burrows below,
  Who died in that fatal fray,
Are resting, unmindful of friend or foe—
  Awaiting the judgment day.
Awaiting the time when the trumpet shall sound,
  And the grave give up its dead,
And garnered by angels, the sleepers around
  In heaven shall be harvested."

—o—

THE ROSE OF SWAKELEY.

Strolling through Swakeley's years agone,
  Ere a care had furrowed my brow,
By the dusty pathway, lying alone,
  In a dismal, dirty slough,
There I saw a flower uprooted lie,
  A miniature wild white rose,
With its little life all parched and dry,
  Fast hastening to its close.

And methought I heard the flower say,
  " Have you never a hand to save ?
Will you pass me by ? alack ! a-day !
  Is there nought for me but the grave ?"

And I turned me back with a sense of shame,
  That 'twere well if the world could see,
And my cheek was suffused with a crimson flame,
  As I raised it tenderly.

Then I bore it away, and pondered how
  I could cherish the fair, frail thing,
And I heard its tremulous voice so low,
  In a piteous whispering,
Saying, " Take me back to my mother, dear,"
  And I reasoned who she could be ;
Was it wind, or rain, or sunshine clear,
  Or a careless wild rose tree?

Then I mused, if to either I give it 'twill die,
  And I know not which calls it its own :
For the wind is at best by a passer-by,
  And the rain but a glassy zone,
And the warm sunshine holds the kiss of death,
  And the tree has no motherly care :
Then I, listening, heard it with bated breath
  Crying out in tones more clear :

" Take me back to her who bore me in pain,
  Take me back to her, or I die—
To my mother, earth, and the wind and rain
  Will be passing presently ;
And the wind will cherish me with its breath,
  And the sunshine come to cheer ;
Any the rain will banish all signs of death,
  And rob me of every fear."

Then I gave the flower to its mother's keep,
  'Neath the shade of a neighbouring tree,
And the sap rose up with a springtide leap,
  And the plant throve valiantly.
And though forty years have passed and gone
  Since I snatched it from where it lay,
The withering plant that I found so lone
  Is a nosegay of smiles to-day.

—o—

THE OLD HOLLOW TREE.

Through the heart of the trunk where the
   life sap once flowed,
  We clambered like sweeps to the crown
Of that old hollow tree that grew out of
   the bank,
  In the lane that leads off from the town;
And seated aloft 'mid its age-shrunken
   limbs,
  How we gabbled and prattled in glee,
Of the grand things we'd do when we
   reached man's estate,
  Far away from that old hollow tree.

Where are all those old friends who then
   seated around,
  Would proclaim the grand deeds they
   would do?
Of the promises made 'mid its whispering
   leaves,
  How many, alas! proved untrue;
Though I looked in each one as I passed
   down the street,
  Not a face in the whole could I see,
Where the sunshine of laughter in ripples
   once ran,
  'Mid the boughs of that old hollow tree.

There's an oak in its prime in the meadow
   beyond
  That was born of an acorn that fell
From the sturdiest limb ere the tree was
   cut down,
  That o'er-shadowed the road in the dell;
And I'm told that in faces I peered in
   to-day,
  There are traces that I failed to see,
Of the once cherished friends who com-
   mingling sat
  On the crown of that old hollow tree.

—o—

BY THE MARGIN OF THE COLNE.

When the clover in full blossom
  Gave its fragrance to the sky,
And the summer winds were singing
  To the winds a lullaby,
I was dreaming, dreaming, dreaming,
  As I wandered on alone,
Of the pleasant days of childhood,
  By the margin of the Colne.

  By the margin of the Colne,
  As I wandered on alone,
  Of the pleasant days of childhood,
  By the margin of the Colne.

What feasts old memories brought me
  As I journeyed by the stream,
How the old joys skipped before me
  In that pleasant old world dream;
And the shouts of joy and laughter
  That once mingled with my own,
Woke once more their sleeping echoes,
  By the margin of the Colne.

  By the margin of the Colne,
  As I wandered on alone,
  Woke once more their sleeping echos,
  By the margin of the Colne.

Like a ruin still I linger,
  Though I'm now three score and three,
And those ever green old memories
  In mine old age comfort me;
Still I feel that I am going,
  As all things before have gone,
Still I'm happy in my old age,
  As I wander by the Colne.

  By the margin of the Colne,
  As I wander all alone,
  I am happy in my old age,
  As I wander by the Colne.

—o—

DOWN WHERE THE MILL-STREAM MEANDERS.

It was down where the mill-stream
   meanders,
  Turning and twisting wherever it will,
Sailing at leisure, dashing at pleasure,
  Down by the mill, down by the mill.

It was there on a bright summer morning,
  Carelessly straying, I wandered alone,
Dreamily musing, watching them cruising,
  Watching the bubbles afloat on the
   Colne.

It was there, turning round, that I saw
   her,
  Tripping along, tripping along;
Light as a fairy, healthful and cheery,
  Trolling a song, trolling a song.

"What are you singing for, maiden?" I asked her,
  "What makes you joyous, dear, as thou'rt fair?"
"Question the thrushes that perch on the bushes,
  Question the birdies everywhere."

It was down where the mill-stream meanders,
  Turning and twisting wherever it will;
Sailing at leisure, dashing at pleasure,
  Down by the mill, down by the mill.

It was there on a bright summer morning,
  Tripping along, tripping along;
From musing awaking, I started love-making,
  Caught by a song, caught by a song.

—o—

CLEAR AS CRYSTAL FLOWS THE COLNE.

Rolling calmly through the meadows,
  Scarce a ripple stirs its breast;
Now and then a few dim shadows
  Shoot across from East to West;
Such is still my native river,
  As it runs its course alone;
Calmly, smooth, unruffled ever,
  Clear as crystal flows the Colne.

Honoured friends, long cherished neighbours,
  As Fate calls you one by one,
May you calmly end your labours
  By the margin of the Colne;
Like your own, my native river,
  Till the sea demands its toll,
May the stream of life for ever
  Flow unruffled to its goal.

—o—

HERNE'S OAK.

Oft I think of the time when a sapling I stood,
And the lands, now unclothed, were all covered with wood;
When the cowslip and primrose sprang up at my feet;
When the shade of my boughs formed a grateful retreat;
When my leaves were the greenest, my limbs stout and strong,
And the birds made my branches a bower of song.
Oft beneath my broad shade hath the light-footed deer
Found a shelter when drowsy, till, startled by fear,
He would dash through the covert t' escape the fleet hound,
While the horn of the hunter re-echoed around.
Over hill and through dale I have viewed, with delight,
The wild chase, till the scene grew bedimmed to the slight;
Then each leaf-stirring blast had no terror for me—
I was King of the Forest—all around me was free!
One midnight, when darkness had shrouded the sky,
When elements warred, and sleet drifted by;
When each cloud, big with anger, rolled over my head,
And Nature seemed striving to waken the dead;
Each flower bowed its head to escape the rude blast,
Each bird crouched with fear as the storm hurried past,
Each bough full of life creaked again and again,
While the wind froze my sap as it ran through each vein.
'Mid the terror and gloom of that terrible night,
At my feet stood the hunter, who, pale with affright,
Sought my boughs, not for safety, for succour, nor shade,
As he'd oft done before while pacing the glade—
His object of search 'mid the elements' strife,
Was death, when all Nature was cringing for life;
And as eager as drowning men struggle for breath,
The hunter sought refuge and quiet in death.
With frenzy-strung nerves he engrasps me around,
With brain changed to fire he springs from the ground,

Till, at length, 'mid my branches, he's dangling high,
And sinks into hell as he climbed to the sky;
While a loud peal of thunder, bursting o'erhead,
Seemed Nature's dread requiem over the dead.
The learned seek me out as I stand here alone,
A memento of actions in ages agone,
When the fattest of calves i' th' forest was found,
Adorned with a buck's head and fairies around;
And each child as he passes beholds me with dread,
While each timid mind pictures rude ghosts of the dead.
My beauty hath faded, no flower at my feet,
No wide-spreading branches, no shady retreat;
All those friends of my youth have long gone to decay.
And I feel that life's tide is fast ebbing away.

—o—

ON THE RUINS OF READING ABBEY.

Thou art far more than the sepulchre
  Of a dark and worn-out creed,
Thou long-wrecked home of learning,
  And of saints whom death has freed.

Who, listless to the strife without,
  In solemn silence wrought,
And garnered the rich fragments
  Of an infant nation's thought.

Full many a kingly-thoughted mind
  Our ancient vessels bore,
From many an eastern nation
  T' illume this darkened shore;

But still 'twas thine own shaven crowns
  These kindred spirits sought,
Who paid the wanderers back in kind
  For golden treasures brought.

When rude hands spoiled thine altars,
  When thy chambers echoed oaths,
They might have spared thy treasures,
  The Vandals and the Goths;

They might have saved from flame and wrack
Those treasures of the mind,
And left untouched the heirlooms
  Of unlettered human kind.

I know thou taught'st an iron creed
  In those benighted days;
That many a sainted foeman died
  'Mid fagots all ablaze:

And in thy dismal dungeons,
  Where day was never seen;
That many a God-like spirit sank
  'Neath torture sharp and keen;

But thy goodness is undying,
  And thine evil passed away,
Like a cloud before the summer sun,
  And night before the day!

—o—

THE GOSPEL OAK.

By the greenwood side where hill meets hill,
Where the parched flowers drink at the fairies distil—
Stands a pollard oak of stalwart mould,
And the green moss clings to its branches old.
Fair Mystery hath a specious charm,
In youth's spring-time, when the heart bloods warm,
And here have strange facts and fictions wove
An altar-piece, and enthroned a love!
A shepherd who tended the flocks in the vale,
Was a living tome of its oft told tale,
And beneath its shade on a summer's day,
In the purple morn or the evening grey,
The villagers thronged with credulous ear,
The oft repeated tale to hear.
He told them of times when thousands came
To hear Christ preach; how the blind and lame
Had won limbs to walk and eyes to see
From the virtuous balm of the Gospel Tree.
He told them the sheep that gambolled around
Were instinctively taught they trod holy ground

And that while in their freedom they branches broke,
They avoided the spell of the Gospel Oak,
And that children who held it a virtue to climb,
Shrank from the tree and were free from all crime;
But the villagers lie 'neath the churchyard stone,
And the shepherd has long to the shepherd gone,
While the tree still laughs at the howling storm,
And bathes in the light of the dewy morn.

—o—

TO MY MOTHER.

I see you yet, dear mother,
    With that wasted boy of mine,
'Mid his long and wakeful sickness,
    In shadowed days lang syne;
In your long and ceaseless watchings,
    As you soothe his fevered brow,
And bid the anxious neighbour
    To whisper yet more low.

When thou thyself wert ailing,
    Thou'dst watch him day and night,
As you sought to quench the fever
    That made his eyes so bright;
And the hand that lifted upward
    My heart untamed and wild,
Was then the shield that parted
    The Conquerer and the child.

When you side by side grew stronger,
    And reached that old elm tree,
Where you fondled o'er my darling,
    As you fondled over me.
You would bear my letter with you,
    Each word of which deceived,
(Ay, still I bless that dear deceit
    For every pain relieved).

In a far off village ale-house,
    I sat me down alone,
For I sought no comfort from a crowd,
    With hearts all turned to stone;
I sat and read your letter,
    With tender heart and true,
And when your eyes shed tears for me,
    My cheeks were wet for you.

—o—

OUR OLD TOWN.

'Tis forty years this very day
    Since I first left the dear old town;
'Twas not my wish to go away,
    And in a strange place settle down:

I loved my home, though e'er so poor,
    I love it yet; it still loves me;
But vessels anchored to the shore
    Are often driven out to sea.

No fair enchantress crossed my path,
    No floating beacon led me on,
No parent banished me in wrath,
    No tyrant bade me to begone.

Whence came the strain, I cannot tell,
    I know its force, and naught beside;
It may have been a sudden swell
    That would not, could not, be denied;

It may have been an adverse wind
    That caught be broadside on, or not,
My puzzled brain can only find
    I drifted from the dear old spot.

How dear to me was that spot then,
    How dearer still has it become;
The roof that shelters little men—
    Is dearer when no longer home.

It may be that my will was weak,
    But will was surely with my love;
I know its strands did never break,
    For each and all were tightly wove.

They may have stretched; but not a strand
    Of that old rope has given way;
The hearts I felt through my right hand
    Still beat for me as yesterday—

Save those whom Death has stricken-down,
    Save those whom I no more shall see;
The friends who dwell in that old town
    Have never lost their love for me.

My love for them has never failed,
    Can never fail while life shall last,
It dances to the freshening gale
    And holds its course amid the blast.

Suspended love of parted friends—
    Is that not living—living still?
'Tis not at graves that true love ends—
    If Life nor Death can never kill.

It lives in its own influence
  Till it shall quicken once again ;
As clouds hold moisture in suspense
  For intervals that know no rain.

Though friends be lost, I feel their love
  Soothing the fretted soul within ;
I feel they watch me from above
  And warn me from the ways of sin.

I see them walk the heavenly plains,
  Come trippingly some steep hill down,
And then, anon, the vision wains,
  But not their love for that old town.

—o—

MY OLD HOME AT UXBRIDGE.

Once more, like a truant, I come back again
  To search for the friendships Ambition betrayed,
To wander through meadow, and village and lane,
  To laugh in the sunshine, and dream in the shade..
My pulse is less free, and the traces of care,
  May be read in the wrinkles that furrow my brow ;
But still there's a magical charm in the air
  That lightens the burden I'm doomed to bear now.

I seek the wild briar I snatched from the grave,
  By Swakeley's old mansion still glimmering bright,
And stretch forth the hand that was stretched forth to save,
  To gather the beauty it filched from the light.
My heart thrills to learn that it flourishes still,
  'Neath the shelter it finds from a neighbouring tree—
It calls up affections no power can kill,
  The love that still lives in the old home for me.

The Gospel Oak still wears a garland of leaves,
  Though its once brawny stem has nigh rotted away ;
Each burrowing root, like an anchor, still cleaves,
  With the grip of despair, to the neighbouring clay.
But where are the legends repeated of yore ?
  They seem to have floated away on the tide,
And the terrible fate is remembered no more
  Of William who broke off a branch for his bride.

The thick-clustered bloom of the old apple tree
  (A garland of beauty to welcome sweet May)
Brings back the bright face of my Bessie to me,
  Its light of love dimming the glories of day.
Her voice is recalled by the silver-toned stream,
  Her neck by the lilies asleep on its breast ;
The brightest of wildings I pluck in my dream
  To grace the rich tresses of her I loved best.

I sit in the shade where we sat long ago,
  Where, Love-taught, I dared to implant the first kiss,
And still I behold the same sun sinking low
  That lingered to steal a last glance of our bliss.
The nightingale's song from the neighbouring grove
  Comes sweeter and clearer across the broad lake ;
Alas ! 'tis the dream of a lingering love,
  And sorrow clings to me the moment I wake.

Still, still, there's a pleasure, though mingled with pain,
  (A pleasure that only the dreamer can taste)
To stroll through these time-treasured scenes once again—

The glow-worms and day-stars of life's
    deary waste.
They call up the pastimes that cloyed us
    of eld,
    Affections that linger though years pass
        away—
The Eden that bound us before we re-
    belled—
    The fount of the fancies we drink of to-
        day.

I call to the echo so prompt to reply,
    Whose voice may be traced by the
        course of the brook,
And, wondering, ask, Will it sicken and
    die,
    Or eternally live in some far-hidden
        nook?
'Tis the same voice to me that I heard in
    the past,
Ring out the rude questions I put to it
    then;
The name of my Bessie, I shout to the
    blast,
And Echo returns to me "Bessie" again.

—o—

BILLY THE SWEEP.

I wish to my heart you'd known Billy,
    That queer little old-fashioned dwarf,
Who used to sleep down in the fell-yard
    By the side of Tom Jenning's wharf;
He slept there in winter and summer,
    Regardless of life's weary load,
A torpid and cold-blooded creature,
    A two-legged leather-skinned toad.

He had only a glimmer of reason,
    It came, and it quickly passed by,
Like the glint of a struggling sunbeam,
    When winter clouds float in the sky.
It would light up his eye for a moment,
    Then vanish, and light it no more,
And leave the on-looker to fancy
    That dim eye was brighter before.

His sides were unshaken by laughter,
    His heart had ne'er bubbled with joy,
He never crossed over the threshold
    That leads to a man from a boy.
No love ever entered his bosom,
    No woman e'er gladdened his sight,
And beauty was only a shadow
    Increasing the darkness of night.

He had no one to love or to hate him,
    And no one to dread or to fear;
Each day and night passed in succession,
    To swell the monotonous year.
Not a feature or fact to remember,
    Cropped up in the long weary way,
No milestone to break up life's journey,
    And sever a year from a day.

He knew of no deep-rooted sorrow,
    No guiltiness harrowed his soul,
And nothing, began and completed,
    Formed part of his life's dreary whole;
The small, narrow world that he moved in
    Was fruitless, and barren and dry,
And the sun, moon, and stars, only span-
    gles
    Affixed to a dull, leaden sky.

But what of that strange little mongrel
    That followed him day after day
And never went far from his shadow
    To gambol, or frolic, or play?
That source of the sole bit of sunshine
    That glinted across the dark road,
And played at Bo-peep like an infant,
    Whenever he wandered abroad.

Did the stream of poor Billy's life ripple
    When the mongrel looked up in his
        face?
Did it sing in unrecognised numbers,
    And joyously quicken its pace?
Did it cast out a spray on its margin,
    And waken new life on its shore?
Or sluggishly move to the ocean,
    Awaiting its presence before.

On the dark winter nights in the fell-
    yard,
    When the piercing winds whistled aloud,
With only a skin wrapped around him,
    He slept like a corse in a shroud.
But watchful and wary and faithful,
    No soul o'er the portal could stir,
Unmarked by his friend and companion,
    Unchallenged by that little cur.

The link that had knit them together,
    That held them for many a day,
Was forged out of love by an angel,
    Who chanced to be passing that way.
Its temper unchanged by the summer,
    Its length unaffected by cold,
'Twas as slim as a gossamer fibre,
    And stronger than iron or gold.

The world has rolled over and over,
  The tide ebbs and flows as before,
And the dew, and the rain, and the sun-
    shine,
  Still comfort the rich and the poor;
But the life of that crude-fashioned
    mortal,
  In spirit and body is free—
The stream with the glimmer of sun-
    shine,
  Is lost in the fathomless sea.

—o—

NOTES TO THE POEMS.

"THE UXBRIDGE TREATY."—On the 30th of January, 1645, the Commissioners of Charles I. and Parliament met, by arrangement, at Uxbridge, in the mansion still known as the "Treaty House," in order, if possible, to end the dispute and Civil war then raging. The Commissioners soon found the impossibility of arranging a treaty to the mutual satisfaction of both parties. After debating for three weeks, the attempt was abandoned, and the King's Commissioners and those of the Parliament separated, each returning to their respective head-quarters. This resulted in a renewal of the Civil war.

"YE WOXBRUGGE TOLLE RIOT."—This riot arose through a dispute between the Town Burgesses and the Countess of Derby, relative to the right to possess and dispose of the proceeds of the market toll. In the law-suit which followed the riot, the Countess established her claim. Heavy fines were imposed upon those who took an active share in the disturbances; but they were afterwards remitted at the instigation of the Countess.

"THE LYNCH MARTYRS."—The special act of martyrdom, upon which the poem is based, was enacted on the site now occupied by the business premises of Messrs. James Leno, Payne, and others, facing the west side of the old burial ground, once known as the Lynch Green. For further particulars of this and similar tragedies on the same spot, see Foxe's "Book of Martyrs."

"THE MOUND ON THE MOOR."—This has now totally disappeared. I remember visiting it some forty years since. It was situated to the west of Cowley Lock, but somewhat nearer Uxbridge. I have no special recollection of its precise form; but to the best of my memory, it did not reach more than a few feet above the plane. I am told by my father, now eighty-six, that in his youth it was much higher. Its history is mere conjecture, though the chances are that it was raised for defensive purposes.

"THE BATTLE OF BULSTRODE."—The early history of Bulstrode is an entire matter of conjecture. That a battle was fought there, I have every reason to believe; but the precise date of the conflict is unknown. Tradition assigns it to the time of the Conqueror. The bull story (I might classify it as the cock and bull story,) is unworthy of belief, and instead of concluding that the bull azure, armed, unguled, ducally gorged and chained, or, in the Somerset arms, has its origin in the story of the Saxons riding to battle on bulls, it would be far wiser to come to the conclusion that the mythical story grew out of the heraldic sign. Those who have read Kingsley's "Hereward-le-Wake" will, I feel convinced, incline to the belief that the story of the battle, as presented in the present poem, is much nearer the truth.

"THE ROSE OF SWAKELEY."—The rose alluded to I picked up and planted beneath a tree, as described, near the pathway that leads from the bridge at the end of the lake to the village of Ickenham, nearly fifty years ago. It was growing vigorously some few years since.

"THE GOSPEL OAK."—This historical remnant of past days is to be seen in the midst of a small clump of trees on the left-hand side of the road to Ickenham. The clump of trees referred to will be found about one hundred yards nearer Ickenham than Cox's, formerly Newdigate's, Lodge.

"THE OLD HOLLOW TREE."—This tree formerly stood in Page's Lane.

MY OLD HOME AT UXBRIDGE.—A shout from the Bridge in Cox's Park will be immediately answered. The shout should be given with the back towards the mansion, in a line with the stream.

PRESS OPINIONS.

It is rather a curious fact that, in spite of the many persons who write verses in their local dialect, we have so few *poems* in the vernacular. Lancashire is, perhaps, the richest of all English counties for poets of the dialect. The strong native speech is rapidly dying out in the cotton county, but concurrently with its decay there has sprung up an extensive literature, the popularity of which is accounted for by its unusual merits. . . . All this brings me to a little book of verse written in the Bucks dialect, and entitled "Kimburton and other Poems." The author is Mr. John Bedford Leno, who attracted attention some time ago by the publication of "Drury Lane Lyrics." The present little work will sustain Mr. Leno's reputation, and will give delight to a large number of readers.—*Newcastle Chronicle*, December 8, 1875.

"Kimburton and other Poems." By J. B. Leno. This book carries its own recommendation on its title-page, and Mr. Leno needs no word of ours to speak for him; he has won his spurs as one of the poets of the poor, and makes one now and then remember Bret Harte. —*National Reformer.*

"Kimburton and other Poems," is by John Bedford Leno, the author of "Drury Lane Lyrics." The poems are spirited and vigorous, with thought underlying them; and they are a plea for the poor and ignorant. There is no political feeling on the surface of these effusions, but it is only necessary to read one or two verses on any page to discover the bent of Mr. Leno's opinions. His pictures of Kimburton are quaint and graphic; and his lines on the "Old and New Parson" are full of fire and animation. We wish we could afford space for the quotation of the poem, which teaches a lesson well worth learning.—*Lloyd's Weekly News*, December 26, 1879.

St. Pancras Working Men's Club.—On Sunday evening last, Mr. John Bedford Leno gave before the members of this club, at their institution in Burton Street, Burton Crescent, under the chairmanship of Mr. Vestryman Robinson, a series of readings of his own most recent metrical productions. Mr. Leno has acquired considerable reputation as one who narrates in verse the "short and simple annals of the poor," and denounces with an anger as righteous the wrongs under which they suffer, as his portraiture of the backward and sad condition of the English agricultural labourer is perspicacious and pathetic. While introducing certain lighter and more playful productions of his muse, the main bulk of Mr. Leno's unpretending but effective readings bore upon our greatest national plague spot, the meagre earnings and consequent bitter lot of the tillers of English soil. His interwoven explanation and illustrative remarks were clear and cogent, and, while delivered with generous warmth, proved in him the presence of practical common-sense, as well as wide and humane sympathies. Himself country bred, many of the representations of facts for which he vouched were warmly re-echoed and confirmed by an audience thoroughly *en rapport* with their entertainer of the evening; and no small section could corroborate from early personal knowledge every utterance which fell from Mr. Leno's lips. At once hearty acquiescence in his statements, and gratitude for the instruction and delight which he had afforded, found unanimous expression in an exceptionally warm vote of thanks.—Nov. 27, 1865.

St. Pancras Working Men's Club.—Considerably more than a score of years ago the name of John Bedford Leno became known to a wide and sympathetic circle of readers of like mind and like heart with himself, by his poetical contributions to the well-known literary column of the *Weekly Dispatch*, of which Eliza Cook was the accredited head And since then, at intervals perhaps not frequent enough, Mr. Leno has kept his hold of the public cognisance and appreciation by various metrical publications, the fruits of his pen. The above club, which is organising and enjoying in a very spirited manner a course of Sunday evening lectures for the current winter, had the advantage, on the last occasion of its assembling for that purpose, of hearing from the lips of Mr. Leno a series of recitations of his most recent effusions. They were almost all concerned with the joys and sorrows—the latter, alas! infinitely predominating—of that still helot class of English labour, from which Mr. Leno informed his audience that he himself sprang, and to the claims and interests of which he has ever remained true and staunch. Forcible extemporaneous elucidations and manly pleadings for his sorely beset clients formed an admirable framework for the recitation of such pieces as "Our Father," "Bet Graham," "Laughing through the soil," etc. But the especial favourite of a large, attentive and heartily enthusiastic audience, was "Grease the Fat Sow," which we very deliberately think Ebenezer Elliot, or even Burns, might have been proud to own as a production. One of the members, in tendering the customary vote of thanks, spoke of Mr. Leno as the poet laureate of the agricultural labour movement. The instantaneous acquiescence of the audience proved their general agreement in the fitness of this eulogistic epithet.—*Labour News*, December 4, 1875.

"The Last Idler, and other Poems." By John Bedford Leno. Mr. Leno, that veteran singer for the people, now offers a considerable poem, with a number of smaller pieces. A tone of energetic aspiration and kindly feeling pervades his pages, and many a true political note rings out in these verses for fellow-toilers. "The Last Idler" is not a continuous exposition, but a series of episodes, representing different aspects of the gospel of work. In the following lines, supposed to be spoken by King Labour, there is undoubtedly a ring of the poet's poet Spenser—

> Go to your homes! this is a day of days,
> And with your joy make all the rafters ring!
> Around each ingle sing your songs of praise,
> And fling aside all sense of suffering;
> Forget old wrongs, nor suffer them to cling,
> And warp the bonds of universal love.
> The winter of the world has changed to spring;
> For this the good in long dark ages strove,
> For this they lived and died, as blood-stained records prove.

—*Weekly Dispatch*, June 30, 1889.

The recent publication of "The Last Idler," a volume of poems by John Bedford Leno, the "Burns of Labour," carries back one's memory to the early fifties, when his first volume, "Herne's Oak, and other Poems," was greeted with great favour by the *Athenæum*, and the literary leaders of the day. In spite of the near approach he has made to the proverbial "three-score years and ten," his poetic eye is by no means dimmed, nor has his right hand lost its cunning. . . Born at Uxbridge in 1826, he was apprenticed to a printer at the age of fourteen, ending his apprenticeship in the stirring times of '48. Already a poet, he soon became known as a fiery speaker, and an active political organizer. About 1856 he became a master printer on his own account, carrying on the business until quite recently, but never slackening meanwhile, as so many would have done, his efforts for the advancement of those who live by labour. With Gerald Massey he started the *Spirit of Freedom*, one of the brightest and most fearless of the dead-and-gone publications whose gravestones serve to mark the path of progress. With many others of these he has been associated, either as editor or as one of the principal contributors. Some of his poems have only lately appeared in the *Commonweal*, between the editor of which paper, Mr. William Morris, and himself there is a strong sympathy and mutual esteem.—*The Political World*, June 15, 1889.

The second edition of " Kimburton ; a Story of Village Life," by John Bedford Leno, will be welcomed by all who appreciate sound sense conveyed in homely verse. Social matters and village politics are happily hit off alike, and the village bard's sympathies are ever with the poor and oppressed.—*Weekly Times*, June 16, 1889.

John Bedford Leno used to be the pleasant political rhymer of days long ago; and a little volume just received shows that his hand has not lost its tuneful touch. "The Last Idler," occupying twenty-seven pages, gives the title to the "fearful tale" he tells "of wrong that labour suffered," and the "theme is labor, famine's deadliest foe." Old Chartists and newer reformers may well turn for an occasional hour to Mr. Leno's lines. Some fifty pages of shorter pieces make up the book. "The Agnostic's Creed" may be commended to Mr. Laing's attention, and we conclude with our songster's profession of faith—

"My creed is love of human kind of every clime and nation,
And on it, though I lose my own, I'd stake the world's salvation."
—*National Reformer*, February 24, 1889.

WORKS by the SAME AUTHOR.

" The Last Idler " - - - - -	**3s. 0d.**
" Drury Lane Lyrics " - - - -	**2s. 0d.**
" Kimburton " - - - - -	**1s. 0d.**
Present Work " The Aftermath " - -	**2s. 0d.**

Post free each 2d. extra.

Address—J. B. LENO,

16, THE LYNCH,

UXBRIDGE, MIDDLESEX.

Please enclose P.O. Order.

www.ingramcontent.com/pod-product-compliance
Lightning Source LLC
LaVergne TN
LVHW061311060426
835507LV00019B/2101